THICK AS THIEVES
London Calling & Dealt With

'In these two short plays, presented at the Theatre Royal, Stratford, East London, in 1981, as a double bill, 'Tony Marchant has given voice to the despair and pent-up rage of an entire generation of unemployed young people . . . With *London Calling*, this immensely talented and perceptive new playwright sets the bleak scene for the explosion which follows: three bright teenagers kick around a patch of East End wasteland without any prospects of work, without any outlet for their hopes and ambitions. In *Dealt With* their sense of impotence and frustration overflows. Making a futile but necessary gesture against the iron economic laws of Thatcherdom, they confront and beard one of the enemy – a sardonic and uncaring Personnel Officer – in his lair.'

Malcolm Hay, *Time Out*

'The thing which ought to hearten the playgoer in search of promising new writers is that Mr Marchant can create such actable characters and give them, within the limits of a lurid vocabulary, an eloquence of their own, and plenty of natural humour.'

Eric Shorter, *Daily Telegraph*

'The mainly naturalistic dialogue is crude, fast and sardonic, and brilliantly captures the rage of their impotence.'

Christopher Edwards, *The Guardian*

'Tony Marchant honestly captures the sad isolation and powerlessness which lies behind the boys' macho bravado and mucking around.'

Dave Robins, *City Limits*

THICK AS THIEVES

LONDON CALLING
&
DEALT WITH

Two Plays by

TONY MARCHANT

A Methuen New Theatrescript
Methuen · London

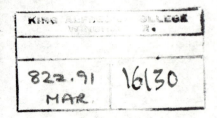
For Margaret

First published as a paperback original in 1982 by Methuen London Ltd,
11 New Fetter Lane, London EC4P 4EE
Copyright © 1982 by Tony Marchant

ISBN 0 413 51070 0

CAUTION
All rights whatsoever in these plays are strictly reserved and application for performance
etc. should be made before rehearsals begin to Harvey Unna & Stephen Durbridge Ltd,
24-32 Pottery Lane, Holland Park, London W11. No performance may be given unless a
licence has been obtained.

LONDON CALLING

London Calling was first presented as part of a double bill with its companion play, *Dealt With,* at the Theatre Royal, Stratford E15, on 13 November 1981, with the following cast:

SAFF	John Fowler
PAUL	Jamie Foreman
PIMPLE	Martin Murphy

Directed by Adrian Shergold
Decor by Jenny Tiramani
Lighting by Gerry Jenkinson
Sound by Simon Curry

A piece of wasteground, walled by corrugated iron. Strewn around: an upturned pram; some old ripped tyres; bits of broken chair; charred wood; a cardboard box; mounds of earth; rubble; bricks. Sometime in July – very hot.
A briefcase is thrown over the wall. SAFF scrambles through a gap in the fence, followed a few moments later by PAUL. Both are breathless.

SAFF (*looking out through the gap in the fence*): Looks all right – can't see nothing.

PAUL: He went down – unconscious . . . or fucking dead.

SAFF: Trust you to look on the bright side.

PAUL: I felt it. He hit his head, cracked it against the pavement.

SAFF: Won't find us here.

PAUL: I've hurt me hand on him. When he fell, he went really still. Limp sort of. Like a doll.

SAFF: I was too busy legging it – I never saw.

PAUL (*screaming*): What if I've fucking killed him!

SAFF (*trying to restrain PAUL from trying to get back through the gap*): No, leave it out – just a black eye and a sore lip. They love it – coppers. He'll be an hero all week. 'Get well' cards, mention in the *Police Gazette* if he's lucky.

PAUL: He was bleeding – look. (*There's blood on his sleeve.*)

SAFF: He hurt you?

PAUL: Cracked me on the back of the head. Stings a bit.

SAFF: Least we got away. (*Pause.*) Nice motor. Nice briefcase. Three litre. Three litre briefcase.

PAUL: He came up all of a sudden.

SAFF: They always do.

PAUL: They'll be swarming about like flies soon. Don't like it when it's one of their own. Kick the shit out of us. Me. When they find me. Police custody – no chance.

SAFF: I don't think he saw our faces.

PAUL: Maybe.

SAFF: All he saw was fist and his life flashing in front of him. It's like *Starsky and Hutch* innit?

PAUL: Is it?

SAFF: Well, no it ain't as it happens, cos the baddies are always no good. (*Pause.*) But we're all right.

PAUL: We'll have to stay here for a bit.

SAFF: Yeah, we picked a nice day for it.

PAUL (*shouting*): Ain't a joke! (*Pause.*) What d'you reckon – if we get done?

SAFF: First offence – for you anyway. Probation Officer with big tits, hairdo and a trenchmac. About 40 – one of them middle-class women with a guilty conscience. Be all right won't it? We can tell her how deprived we are. Never been shown no affection or nothing. Never had Christmas presents. Yeah, all that.

PAUL: Terrific.

SAFF is trying to get the briefcase open.

SAFF: They don't put you away no more – they got these new ideas. You have to spend so many hours doing something for the community – like decorating old people's homes, doing gardening, sweeping up leaves in the park.

PAUL: What park? Ain't no park round here. No leaves either. No fucking trees – or gardens. So how can you do gardening?

SAFF: All right, all right! They was just examples. Examples. Colin Reeve had to help do the big painting at some youth club in Bow when he got done for burglary. Big painting on the wall outside.

PAUL: Mural.

SAFF: Yeah, I was just going to say that. Anyway, it's all for the community ain't it? This new idea they got. Sounds like a doddle eh? Better than doing cross country runs round some borstal in Slough or wanking yourself silly in a remand centre for two months.

PAUL: He sort of curled up when he was on the floor dribbling blood and spit. His face was all contorted. I just hit out y'know – when he whacked me. Just defending meself y'know. They won't see it that way. (*Pause.*) Or they might just give us a fine, yeah.

SAFF: They ain't caught us yet. And they ain't going to. Fuck me, you're a gloomy bastard sometimes.

PAUL: Head feels a bit raw. Can you see anything?

SAFF (*looking*): Nah – only dandruff.

PAUL: Bit unreal – all that happening.

SAFF: Can't get this fucking thing open. (*Bashing the briefcase against the floor.*)

PAUL *comes over, pushes* SAFF *out of the way, opens the catch, walks away.*

PAUL: Anything in there?

SAFF (*pulling out items*): Travel brochure, ruler, keys . . .

PAUL: What sort?

SAFF: Front door keys I think. (*Pause.*) Bleeding file in here.

PAUL: Great – I'll do me nails.

SAFF: No – not that sort of file. Business file. (*He pulls it out.*) 'A New Way'.

PAUL: What?

SAFF: 'A New Way – Plans for Dockland.' Lot of drawings, pages of writing. (*Pause.*) Says something here about having an art gallery . . .

PAUL: Let's have a look.

SAFF: Hold on. (*Pause.*) And a yachting marina. That's nice innit – I been looking for somewhere to put my yacht ain't you? It's a bleeding nuisance having to keep it in me bedroom. Wait till I tell me mum about the art gallery. She'll be all excited. Better than bingo innit? (*He throws the file to* PAUL.) Drawing of an hotel and shops and stuff there. Limehouse, I think it says. They got a map. Can't understand why they wanna build an hotel there, can you? Bit like having a wine bar in the middle of a cemetery. Might be some jobs going there through.

PAUL: Yeah – we can be bell boys.

SAFF: Carry your luggage sir.

PAUL: Get a two bob tip.

SAFF: Geezer whose motor it was must have been a businessman. Would have had the cassettes if that copper hadn't showed up. Only reason I got the door open. Thought there might have been something in the briefcase. How you supposed to make your way in life with coppers jumping on ya?

PAUL (*mildly sarcastic*): Show a bit of initiative and what d'you get?

SAFF: Yeah, show a bit of what you just said and all we end up with is a fucking briefcase. D'you think we can knock it out somewhere?

PAUL: Who'd want to buy a briefcase round here. You don't know any businessmen along your landing do ya? Businessmen don't live round here – they just come down from the City in their flash motors with all this. (*He throws the file.*)

SAFF: It might be leather though.

PAUL *stares at him.*

I'll use it meself – evening classes like.

PAUL *has been flicking through the briefcase. He throws it.*

PAUL: Nice here innit? D'you come here often?

SAFF: Well, it's in its early stages innit? But you just wait – give the Council two brooms and a Friday afternoon – and this shitheap you see before you will be transformed into a sauna solarium, running track, a new national football stadium, church and bingo hall with an olympic sized swimming pool.

PAUL: For the local community, like.

SAFF: That's it. (*Pause.*) It's going to be a ski resort as well.

PAUL: Where they going to get the snow?

SAFF: Grow it, won't they? Grow it in Kent.

Pause.

PAUL: Stay here for a bit then.

SAFF: Our hide-out.

PAUL: He was bleeding. He come up all of a sudden. I had to hit him. That's assault innit?

SAFF: Yeah, assault and vinegar. Look, no one was about, he won't be able to remember what we looked like and I been at home all day watching *Emmerdale Farm*.

PAUL: He hit me first . . . but that don't

matter does it? (*He feels his head.*)
There's no bump there . . . just a bit sore.

SAFF (*laughing*): Victor Romeo in pursuit,
over. Two suspects armed with a
briefcase – approach with caution, over –
highly dangerous Victor Tango.

PAUL: He'll remember me. I know. Well,
they make a job out of it don't they?

SAFF: Yeah – they're highly trained – just
like their dogs. (PAUL *eases, smiles.*) All
round athletes they are, running,
jumping and arresting.

PAUL: Linking arms. Standing up in court.

SAFF: I told him it was a silly place to put
his groin your honour.

PAUL: In my knee your honour.

SAFF: Bruises? What bruises? He must
have slipped on the stairs your honour,
when me boot found its way up his arse.

PAUL: I'm a family man your honour.

SAFF: I don't even mind dancing with the
spades during the Notting Hill carnival
your honour.

PAUL: Give him six months.

SAFF: For assaulting a policeman your
honour. (*Pause.*) Yeah, if the meat
wagon shoots up here, they better be
wearing their crash helmets. They'll be
sorry they ever took the pledge.

PAUL: Why – what you going to do?

SAFF: I'm going to take you hostage ain't I?

PAUL: Oh dear.

SAFF: They'll be shitting themselves.
Trying to look all efficient and calm for
the TV cameras. They'll be pleading with
me through the loudspeakers and I'll be
sending out my demands.

PAUL: What demands?

SAFF: I'll draw up a list. Helicopter to East
Ham. Sandwiches and coffee.

PAUL: They'll try and put something in the
coffee.

SAFF: I'll have two sugars.

PAUL: No, wanker. Drugs. To put you to
sleep.

SAFF: Oh well, as you're going to be my
hostage, you can be the guinea pig as well.
First sip. (*Pause.*) You got to have big feet
to get in the police.

PAUL: And a blue anorak that don't fit,
with Tesco flared jeans when you're off
duty.

SAFF: S'funny innit – no one from round
here ever joins the police.

PAUL (*dryly*): Amazing.

SAFF: Perhaps no one round here is five
feet eight. It's all them lanky middle-class
wankers from Finchley, that join the
police. The ones that was prefects at
school. Play rugby and grow moustaches
and have nurses for girlfriends.

PAUL: Police are cunts. Hate the fucking
police . . . hate. (*Very thoughtful and very
painful.*) I remember . . . bastards. Me
dad . . . a few months before he died . . .
used to get attacks . . . got a bit funny.
Tremble like, get confused. Pressure on
his brain doctors said . . . fucking tumour.
Coming home from work one day . . . it
happened to him . . . had an attack sort of
. . . got lost . . . wandering about, pain in
his head. He was 45, hands like fucking
boxing gloves, used to like a drink . . .
took me fishing . . . he knew things me
dad . . . shrewd. (*Pause.*) Anyway, old bill
found him . . . wandering about near the
canal . . . like a kid . . . little boy . . . his
trousers all wet . . . pissed himself . . .
couldn't remember nothing. Cunts tried
to nick him . . . drunk and disorderly . . .
empty out his pockets at the station . . .
poor sod didn't know what day it was.
Drunk and disorderly they tried to pull
. . . me and me mum had to go and collect
him. They didn't apologise. Unfortunate
incident they said. (*Pause.*) He was all
right usually. (*Disgusted.*) Drunk and
fucking disorderly. (*Pause.*) Morphine
and radium . . . till he died. (*Pause.*)
Bastards . . . bastards . . .

A long awkward silence.

SAFF: That's fucking bad that is. (*Pause.*)
Yeah . . . anyone wants to join the Old
Bill has to go to a special place just
outside Hendon . . . go on a special six
month training course to learn how to
switch their fucking walkie talkies on.

PAUL (*still a little preoccupied through
recovered slightly*): Animals like us have
to be kept off the streets.

SAFF: Yeah . . . by animals in uniforms.

*Pause. PAUL wipes his forehead with his
sleeve.*

PAUL: Hot.

SAFF: What?

PAUL: Hot.

SAFF: Who, you?

PAUL: And it.

SAFF: It what?

PAUL: Hot.

SAFF: Oh. (*Pause.*) Yeah, is a bit.

PAUL (*smiling*): Bit what?

SAFF (*serious*): Hot. (*Pause.*) Waste of fucking time the sun shining round here.

PAUL: It's been ordered to.

SAFF: Who by?

PAUL: The Government. It's the Government's idea. The sun goes round all the piss-hole areas of the country, making special guest appearances – mostly in July. Cheer everyone up like. Keep up our morale.

SAFF: Our what?

PAUL: Our morale. It's the Government's idea. Shine down there on that council estate for a bit, they said, then do that street with all the houses boarded up. Where the meths drinkers live. Let everyone have a bit of sun. Keep the natives happy, they said, show your face – out everyone'll come in their T-shirts and sunglasses looking for the ice-cream man.

SAFF: Very clever that is.

PAUL: It's touring the country.

SAFF: Bit like the queen.

PAUL: But it don't do evening functions.

SAFF: Me trousers are stuck to me legs. All sweaty. Like fucking superglue.

PAUL: I remember the day before the queen came down here for the Jubilee – council came and painted the garage doors, put fences up round where the docks used to be and laid a bit of turf in the grounds of the flats.

SAFF: Yeah, that's right – they stuck little toy trees along the pavement and cleaned all the writing off the walls, and hung banners everywhere.

PAUL: It looked really nice for a change.

SAFF: And then they took it all back soon as she left.

PAUL: Did you see her? The queen I mean.

SAFF: Nah. Me and me mate from school was too busy trying to nick camera gear out the BBC van.

PAUL: She went into the town hall with the mayor. Loads of people all jostling to have a look, to see her. I was only thirteen.

SAFF: I heard she got out of the car, had one look at what she'd come to visit and went 'fuck this'. Pissed off back to Buckingham Palace.

PAUL: She didn't visit nothing. Only the mayor, like. Then she got back in the Rolls. Right flash, with flags on it. She was waving.

SAFF: No, I bet she was doing this. (*Tossing gesture.*)

PAUL: 'I am a dull and simple lad and I have never met the queen.'

SAFF: Eh?

PAUL: David Watts. The Jam sing that. And 'Meet me on the Wasteland'. For places like this.

SAFF: Yeah . . . this is the sort of place where the Clash used to have their picture taken. Urban something innit?

PAUL: Lot of spaces like this round here. (*Holding the keys in his hand, rattling them. Pause.*) Geezer with the briefcase probably got a house backing onto a golf course. We got this.

SAFF: My nan used to live here – before they knocked it all down. Ages ago. I'm probably standing on where her front room used to be. If you see any wallpaper with daisies on it – that's from her bedroom.

PAUL: Probably find the remains of some old couple who didn't want to move and who got run over by the council bulldozers and bured alive.

SAFF: Oh you poet! You're a fucking poet you are! You got a wonderful imagination! You don't half come out with some things sometimes Paul. Sometimes, I can't work you out. Like when you go off on your own and we don't see you for days. If you didn't get dragged out by me and the others – you probably wouldn't hang around with us.

PAUL: I don't go anywhere – I ain't got no country cottage or nothing. I stay in me bedroom a lot – just listening to me LPs. That's all.

SAFF: That's your story – boys in their bedrooms, I know what goes on.

PAUL: Course you do. No right. I put on Setting Sons or something – get a right buzz listening, right high. Sort of excited, like. Shut everything else out. All the noises in the flats – people arguing, toilets flushing, cars revving up. I don't hear nothing except what I wanna hear. Hours I spend listening and smoking. It's like there ain't nothing else that's true except what they're saying. Paul Weller – he writes terrific songs. He really knows what's going on – how you feel, like. (*Pause.*) What we going to do if they come?

SAFF: Who – Old Bill? Er. . . (*Looking puzzled, then smiling.*) Run like fuck.

PAUL: What I done to that copper, it's bad innit, it's serious. If I get caught . . . I didn't mean . . . oh fuck it. If you hit a copper, it's worse innit? In the interview room . . . it's just you and them right? Kick me head in. (*Pause.*) Got a pain, throbbing in me nut.

SAFF: I reckon you should go up the hospital.

PAUL (*shouting*): No! It's nothing much.

SAFF: I get a bit of a throb. Especially in summer.

PAUL: Why's that?

SAFF: All the birds . . . the way they dress. All revealing like. No bras and thin T-shirts and see-through dresses and flesh coming out all over, everywhere you look – tits and bums and thighs. Yeah, I get a definite throb. I bet a lot of wanking goes on in summer. I always seem to find a lot of stains on my trousers in summer.

PAUL: I bet your mum keeps running out of cooking oil.

SAFF: That's why I know what goes on in boys' bedrooms. Anyway, margarine's best. And Oil of Ulay. I use me mum's. Me sister asked me what I wanted for me birthday. A big bottle of Oil of Ulay I says. She says what about some aftershave. You're fucking joking I says –

I can't use that. She think it's cos I got sensitive skin. (*Pause.*) I wanna toss it off, not burn it off.

PAUL: Just as well you don't make model aeroplanes – she might have bought you a tube of Bostik.

SAFF: I should get the Nobel Prize for my services to wanking. Me and me wrist are getting engaged. Aladdin's lamp between me legs. On the bog, in the bath, on the top deck of the bus, into my shoe, up the garage wall and down the alley. I got blisters on my hands. Some people play Space Invaders . . .

PAUL: And you shake hands with your best friend.

SAFF: Thumb a lift. Mum comes into my bedroom, she says 'Smells funny in here'. That's sweat mum I says, hot in here, I says. That's where I been sweating. She keeps spraying air freshener in there.

PAUL: That right? You wanna find a nice girl.

SAFF: I wouldn't mind settling down with a box of Kleenex. (*Pause.*) I don't fancy getting old though. I mean, like getting arthritis in me hands. All me fingers all stiff and curled up. I'd be fucked then, wouldn't I? Yeah – being old – can't even Midland Bank properly, can you?

PAUL: There's this old woman couple of doors along from us – only moved in a couple of weeks ago – on her own like. Someone found her the other night – running along the balcony in her nightdress – two o'clock in the morning. She'd been running up and down the landing shouting. She kept saying something about her garden . . . like she seemed to think someone had nicked it or something . . . she was dead certain.

SAFF: Was she looking for it then?

PAUL: Dunno . . . sort of. She must have gone a bit funny . . . too much for her, moving and that. Took her to hospital.

SAFF: Gotta be a fucking cross-country champion to run up and down your landing. How many doors are there?

PAUL: About fifty from one end to the other.

SAFF: Fucking postman must be on steroids to do your estate.

PAUL: She kept saying about it. Bit weird innit? In her nightdress – two o'clock in the morning. She must have had a garden once or something.

SAFF: We was going to have a window box in our place – but we didn't realise – we ain't got no windows. Me dad wanted to try and grow some tomatoes – now he's bought some plastic fruit. (*Pause.*) Don't taste as nice as what we used to have.

PAUL: That why you got such a rosy complexion?

SAFF: No, that's cos I use Camay.

PAUL: Your cheeks . . . colour of piss.

SAFF: I thought they was more of a dirty grey colour meself. So I can camouflage meself in the alleys, in the lifts and on the garage roof. It's like the soldiers wearing green in the jungle or secret agents blacking up their faces at night – well, I'm dirty grey in Plaistow. Same sort of thing. Mingle without being noticed. Natural colours of my . . . of my . . . what d'you call it?

PAUL: Environment.

SAFF: Yeah, like them animals. Chamois leathers or something.

PAUL: How d'you manage to perfect this disguise then?

SAFF: What – my dirty grey look you mean?

PAUL: Yeah.

SAFF: Simple innit – I don't wash. I don't wash and I hang around where the cars are parked and stick me face in front of the exhaust pipes. I've given up washing. I've retired.

PAUL: Soap's a dirty word then.

SAFF: I wish I'd said that.

PAUL: So what do you do then?

SAFF: I smell. I smell very badly. Stink the place out. Once, I used to be able to flash my armpits on trains.

PAUL: You had that built-in confidence.

SAFF: I used to be the one that told his best friend he had BO.

PAUL: It must have been catching.

SAFF: I remember getting ready for me sister's wedding – I had a bath, even washed off the dirt between me toes. It was the cleanest I'd ever been. Combed me hair, brushed me teeth and pulled the fluff out me foreskin.

PAUL: Special occasion.

SAFF: Then I sprayed myself under the armpits like and up me bum with anti-perspirant.

PAUL: Right.

SAFF: I'd picked up the wrong can. Fucking fly killer weren't it?

PAUL: No flies on you.

SAFF: It must have been good stuff though – I didn't sweat all day. Just felt a bit dizzy. Fell over once or twice.

PAUL: How d'you get on at your sister's wedding?

SAFF: All right – me carnation wilted though. I was dancing with me cousin. She wanted to know what the funny smell was. I told her it was my Moroccan aftershave. A bottle of duty free. Dead expensive like.

PAUL: Dancing with you – I bet she went all weak at the knees.

SAFF: Yeah, especially when she got a whiff of my Moroccan aftershave. She had to be took out the hall. She come over all funny.

PAUL: It's like putting talcum powder all over yourself and then finding out it's Ajax. (*Pause.*) Quiet. No sirens or nothing. Probably coming over on the police radio . . . about us like. Two youths. That's what they call us innit? Youths. That's the police's way of saying teenage scum.

SAFF: If you was working for Barclays Bank they'd call you a young adult.

PAUL: Ain't bad enough we have to live in filing cabinets anyway, without them giving us a name, giving us a fucking title. Youths. I know I'm something else first. (*Pause.*) The way he went down Saff . . . hurt me hand. Had to get away though right?

SAFF: If we'd got done, it's two offences . . . but I don't reckon there'll be any comeback. If they're supposed to be looking for two youths seen breaking into a car and all that – I mean, that's half the fucking kids in London.

PAUL: But they know what area we come from. They know we come from round here.

SAFF: They don't know us from Adam. It ain't PC Plod on the beat no more, tell our mothers to smack our arses. It ain't some jolly copper standing on a street corner saying who's been naughty boys then.

PAUL: It never has been.

SAFF: Well, like you said they're after two youths with a briefcase and one of them has got a sore head resisting arrest. That's all they know.

PAUL: But if he remembers me face.

SAFF: Look, don't worry about no identity parades all right? Living around here, we ain't got a face, we're . . . what's the word?

PAUL: Anonymous.

SAFF: That's it . . . anonymous. Lovely summer we're having. My geraniums are coming on a treat.

Pause.

PAUL: Summer . . . gets on me nerves a bit. Big blue skies . . . all them dads on the adverts watering their lawns. Yeah, summer makes things seem worse . . . more crowded together, all the people in the flats. And when you got nothing to do, nowhere to go . . . you notice it more.

SAFF: Tell you what I noticed.

PAUL: What's that?

SAFF: According to *News at Ten* I'm disaffected. What's that mean . . . is it like being disinfected?

PAUL: Probably just means you're fed up.

SAFF: I'm fed up we only nicked this briefcase. Here Paul, fancy going on holiday?

PAUL: Where we going?

SAFF: Malta looks nice. It tells you all about it here. (*Pause.*) Malta. (*Reading from the brochure.*) This small island lying as far south as Tunisia's Sousse has a warm, welcoming heart, for the friendly Maltese have always been very much at home with the British. It is an island of low, rolling hills and terraced fields, of golden stone towns and grandly domed baroque churches; and island bordered by a coastline of sandy bays, high cliffs and a sea of the clearest, deepest turquoise. (*Pause.*) Says here it's got a lot of individual charm. Don't mention the flies though. I bet there's loads of flies – why don't it say nothing about the flies?

PAUL: That's cos they all died at your sister's wedding. You killed 'em all off with your Moroccan aftershave.

SAFF: What about Sicily? (*Reading inaudibly something similar about Italy.*)

PAUL (*talking to SAFF who isn't really listening*): Only place we're going is in the lifts in the flats – from the ground floor to the fifth. Smell the piss on the way up. (*Pause.*) Days like this . . . makes me feel closed in . . . and if you get out to go up the West End or Hyde Park or somewhere, you always knows that you have to come back, come back here. There's such a lot of things I wanna do with me life y'know.

SAFF (*reading aloud*): Cultural crossroads of Europe and Africa. Here Paul, what's an azure sea?

PAUL: Dunno. (*Pause.*) Jam got a song called 'In the City'. Reminds me of things. (*Longer pause.*)

SAFF: You're too bleeding quiet sometimes – I don't know what you're thinking. You ain't got a big mouth like the rest of us. Things cut deep with you – I noticed.

PAUL: This is my life – I'm blushing.

SAFF (*thumbing through the brochure*): I think I prefer Malta. Girls in that picture had bigger tits. Shall I go and book up then? (*They stare at each other saying nothing.*) Don't wanna go abroad anyway – loads of bloody Germans drinking Double Diamond, eating fish and chips and putting their towels over all the deckchairs.

PAUL: How d'you know?

SAFF: Me sister's just come back from Benidorm – that's how I know. No, we'll stay in East London and get savaged by guard dogs or nick briefcases.

PAUL: If you put an animal in a cage right – it'd try and bite through the bars to get out at first.

SAFF: So what?

PAUL: I reckon we're like them animals sometimes. In a sort of cage, like. 'Cept we smash things up but we ain't getting out. It's easy to wreck what's ugly and shitty, what shadows you all the time. All round here. Smash it up, set light to it, write all over it, piss on it. That's what it deserves.

SAFF: Vandals.

PAUL: That's what makes me laugh. Getting called vandals – for smashing up what no one wants anyway. What's just there, decaying. Ain't as if there's anything round here to care about. Respect. Nothing round here that belongs to us, see – that we can look after and be proud of. They've never built fuck all for us, done nothing for us. They just put warning signs up everywhere, telling us what we can't do and corrugated iron round everything. (*He picks up a milk crate, throws it against the wall. Pause.*) Oh! Glass splinters in me head – cutting.

SAFF: Paul – you all right? Paul? What the fuck did he hit you with – Tower Bridge? (*Pause.*) Here, I saw this student on the tube yesterday. I thought he was having a fight with someone. Turns out he was trying to get his rucksack off. Always travelling about though ain't they, students? Always hitching round Europe or something. (*Pause.*) Heatwave innit?

PAUL: Me back's all wet, sticky. It's sweltering, must be about 90. Think I'll take me shirt off. (*He does so.*) Catch the sun. Tell the Old Bill that's what I been doing all day. If they come. Be a sort of alibi.

SAFF: You won't get no suntan – you'll get some skin disease, you'll get rust.

PAUL: Sky's burning. Must be an heat haze all over London . . . shimmering. All the windows all . . . shining . . . all reflecting the sun.

SAFF: You'll get lead in your veins.

PAUL (*putting his shirt on floor, lies on it*): I can imagine I'm somewhere else.

SAFF: Contaminated.

PAUL: I went to Folkestone once. With me mum and dad . . . for a week . . . Walking on the beach . . . see for miles you could. Skimming stones . . . four bounces on the water. Brilliant it was . . . so quiet . . . sea was massive. Walked for ages . . . sand between me toes.

SAFF: I went to Brighton once. It pissed down with rain and me candy floss went all soggy.

PAUL: You look more handsome with a tan.

SAFF: Who says?

PAUL: It's well known. Women like men who've been bronzed and touched by the sun. Virile looking, healthy like. Brings out their . . . instincts.

SAFF: What instincts?

PAUL: Their primitive desires. Makes 'em uncontrollable – that dark, continental look – it's romantic.

SAFF: Oh yeah – like Omar Sharif or Sacha Distel . . . (*Unbuttoning his shirt.*) I can tell everyone I been to the South of France . . . all the girls, they like a bit of the old Mediterranean (dump) look. (*Looking up and shouting.*) Bronze me! Bronze me! Here . . . am I brown yet? (*He laughs.*) You've been exposed to my sweaty body – you've got two minutes to live.

PAUL: Worse than a nuclear explosion.

SAFF: You're going to be all disfigured and horrible in a minute.

PAUL (*climbing the wall*): It'll be on the news. (*Looking out over the wall.*)

SAFF: 'Most of East London was today evacuated from their homes when a young man who hadn't washed for three weeks took his shirt off. Road blocks have been set up and the Army has been called in.'

PAUL (*sees something*): Jesus – we got bother now!

SAFF: What's the matter?

PAUL: Old Bill – that's what's a matter!

SAFF: Oh shit and piss!

PAUL: Stay down you cunt! Stay down!

SAFF: I gotta have a look ain't I?

PAUL: We can't run or they'll see us. I knew it!

SAFF: It ain't my fault is it!

PAUL: I ain't blaming you, all right!

SAFF: You sure you hid that briefcase?

PAUL: Course I'm fucking sure! (*Running to hide it more thoroughly.*)

SAFF: Don't panic.

PAUL: We been sunbathing right? All day, we been here all day!

SAFF: Terrific.

PAUL: Think of something better then, smartarse!

SAFF: Looks worse if we hide. Looks fucking suspicious. Get a fag out – make it look casual. Mind you – this ain't very fucking casual is it? Hurry up then!

PAUL: All right!

SAFF: How come there's only one?

PAUL: D'you want me to ask 'em why or something? (*Pause.*) I've hit one of his mates – there'll be others behind and they'll wanna hurt me – they'll say it's what I deserve. They don't have to make excuses no more Saff, not after what's been happening.

SAFF: He's coming this way.

PAUL: We don't know nothing about no car right! Right!

SAFF: I can't see him wearing a uniform.

PAUL: What is he – white shirt and black tie?

SAFF: What d'you want – a fashion show or something?

PAUL: They'll wanna make an example of me. Don't you understand, you cunt!

SAFF: He's carrying something.

PAUL: Tooled up. They can do that now.

SAFF: Oh fucking hell!

PAUL: What you doing? (*Pause.*) What a joke. From a distance I thought . . . I thought . . .

SAFF: I know what you thought.

PAUL: Couldn't know for certain though, right? I mean . . . oh shit . . had to make sure. They must be out patrolling . . . in their rovers . . . out looking.

SAFF (*shouts*): Oi Pimple! Got your truncheon with ya! Paul here has just done macaronis in his pants!

PAUL: Just shut up, right!

PIMPLE *scrambles through. He is wearing a tracksuit top, holding a football.*

PIMPLE: Hello Paul, all right?

PAUL: What the fuck you doing here!

PIMPLE: Why – what's a matter?

SAFF: Ever had an electrical current passed through your balls, Pimple? Ever been forced to swallow a sandbag? Ever had dyno-rod stuck up your arse?

PIMPLE: No – what you talking about?

SAFF: Pain. Unbearable pain. You'll have to smell my BO as punishment. What you doing over here anyway? No one comes over here.

PIMPLE: I've only come to see if there's anywhere I can have a game. Who did you think I was anyway? Someone after you?

PAUL: S'all right Pimple – we thought you was someone else. (*Pause.*) Didn't see any Old Bill about did you? In the streets like? Asking questions?

SAFF: Taking down particulars. In their notebook.

PAUL: That's right.

PIMPLE: Why – they after you! You nicked something? What you got! Let's have a look! Let's have some!

SAFF: Don't go mad Pimple, don't have a fit. Don't go all epileptic on us. He was only asking.

PAUL: Just wanted to know Pimple, that's all.

SAFF: Here – d'you bring my Ambre Solaire with you?

PIMPLE: What's that?

SAFF: To rub on me body. (*Pause.*) See the deep manly chest I've carved out for meself. Me biceps bulge and me thighs ripple. You too could have a body like mine.

PAUL: If you're not careful.

PIMPLE: You're a headcase.

SAFF: Son, they used to call me toastrack at school – because my ribs used to stick out. And now I'm all dynamic. I sent off for one of them bullworkers to make a man of me. I was so excited when the postman came – but I couldn't use it.

PIMPLE: Why's that?

SAFF: Cos I couldn't get the fucking box open.

PIMPLE: Why you two got your shirts off?

PAUL: Fun – ain't you ever had none?

SAFF: We've just been on the floor.

PIMPLE: What – together?

SAFF: And now you've found us. Half naked. Now you know our secret. We thought we'd be safe here. Secluded place, no one about.

PIMPLE: Go way! You're winding me up! (*Unsure, proferring the ball.*) Here, see how long you can keep it up. I done forty-eight yesterday. C'mon don't mess about.

SAFF: I want you, Pimple.

PIMPLE: What for?

SAFF: An orgy. Arms and legs and bums and bad breath. Let's make a baby.

PIMPLE: Shut up dirtbox.

SAFF: Here – on my head! (PIMPLE *throws him the ball.*)

PIMPLE: See . . . queers don't like football . . . if you was bum chums . . . you wouldn't like football.

PAUL: Yeah, all that spitting and ralgex and chewing gum and hairspray. You're right, it's definitely a man's game.

PIMPLE: Course it is. Nowhere to play round here though. They've pulled everything down.

PAUL: No good here. It's all broken glass and bricks and dog shit.

SAFF: Reminds me of my front room.

PIMPLE: I used to come over here a lot . . . with the others. We used to come and build bonfires. Took us ages to set 'em up. Great to see it all go up.

PAUL: Us as well. Our heritage – building things with rubbish and setting light to 'em. (*Pause.*) Wrong time of the year for football innit Pimple? Closed season.

PIMPLE: Ain't never the wrong time of year for football.

SAFF: You can make out you're playing in the fourth division. They got pitches like this.

PIMPLE: No pitches round here. If it weren't for *Match of the Day* I wouldn't know what grass looked like. But I thought if I cleared some of the bricks out the way, put bits of wood over where the holes are . . . I could have a game up against that fence. Don't rebound properly though does it?

PAUL: You wanna find somewhere flat.

SAFF: My sister's chest – that's flat.

PIMPLE: Didn't think I'd see anyone over here. (*Pause.*) So what d'you nick then? What d'you get?

SAFF: We didn't get nothing. Tell a lie. Paul got something. (SAFF *looks at* PAUL.)

PIMPLE: Where you been then?

PAUL: Car spotting.

PIMPLE: If they're after you – why d'you come over here?

PAUL: First place we could think of running. Out the way, like.

SAFF: If you'd brought the ambre solaire. with ya, I could have emptied a bottle out over meself. With my white arms and legs I'd look like spaghetti in tomato sauce.

PAUL (*to* PIMPLE): Scouts'll be round after you soon, sign you up . . . apprenticeship. Signing the forms, shaking hands with John Lyall. Picture in the paper.

SAFF: Only scouts he'll see'll be the ones rubbing two sticks together.

PIMPLE: If I keep working on me basic skills . . . I'll get in a team that plays Sunday mornings. Me passing – that's me biggest weakness. That's all that lets me down.

Pause.

PAUL: Hottest it's been for ages. Baking. Melt all the buildings away . . . all the tower blocks, our estate . . . all melt away to nothing in the heat. Make some space for everyone. Be great.

PIMPLE: Buildings can't melt. (*To* SAFF:) What's he talking about?

SAFF: He's imagining. He's been doing a lot of that today. He's got a wonderful imagination.

PAUL: Shit. (*Trying to control the ball.*)

SAFF: Where?

PAUL: Me. Can't play.

PIMPLE: Ball bounces different on grass.

SAFF: That right?

PIMPLE: Yeah, different. I played on grass a couple of times – when I got in the school team. Always had to play away though cos they never had a pitch. I played at Tooting once. Brilliant it was. Brilliant playing on grass it is. Slide tackles, run thirty yards down the wing . . . diving headers. All the proper markings on it. Half way line and all that. (*Pause.*) They got goalposts at Hackney Marshes, but you have to get a bus and it takes twenty minutes. Can't do diving headers on me landing can I?

SAFF: Council's idea of doing something for kids round here is to put a ping pong table in the adventure playground – and that ain't even got a net. (*Pause.*) D'you know what the easiest way to commit suicide in Newham is? Jump out your kitchen window.

PIMPLE: What if you don't live in a tower block?

SAFF: D'you wanna know another way of getting killed instantly?

PIMPLE: What's that?

SAFF: Messing my jokes up you little bastard! (*Pause.*) Here Pimple, you a virgin?

PIMPLE: Course not – I ain't never been.

SAFF: What d'you do then – tell us all the details.

PIMPLE: Well, I always smoke a cigarette after and I say, 'How was it for you?'

PAUL: Saff's dad smokes a cigarette before, during and after.

SAFF: Yeah, and when he asks me old dear what it was like, she says, 'Dunno, couldn't see what was going on with all that bleeding smoke'.

Pause.

PAUL: I wonder what's happened – to that copper. How long we been here you reckon?

SAFF: Too long.

PIMPLE: Was it a young copper?

SAFF: Yeah, one of them enthusiastic bastards just out of Hendon. Them young ones are really flash, they think they've got something to prove. If they see you with a rolled up Daily Mirror they wanna nick you for having an offensive weapon. They think they're authority. They're just boys with acne.

PAUL: Living round here y'know – it's like you're caught inside a clenched fist. I tell you something – dolphins have got it sussed.

SAFF (*a bit incredulous*): What?

PAUL: Dolphins. I was watching this documentary about 'em. They got it sussed. Swimming under oceans together. Not swimming, gliding. They can go anywhere, always be in control of their world. A world of water and they own it and play in it. Did you know dolphins play games? In the middle of seas all over the world they play games. Finding food everywhere and being together. No worries. Just thinking and gliding across oceans . . . long, smooth bodies. Free. Oh Jesus – we gotta go somewhere, we gotta get away from here!

SAFF: Flipper was a dolphin – on the telly. He used to make this silly noise like those little dolls make when you press their stomachs in. Some soppy kid used to be his friend – he was called Ricky or something.

PIMPLE: Yeah and he used to lean over the boat and stick this hooter in the water. Right stupid I thought.

Pause.

PAUL: They'll be in shirt sleeves, the Old Bill. If they come, like. It being hot.

SAFF: Yeah, sucking ice-lollies. And the dogs'll be wearing sunglasses.

PAUL: Don't get flash, all right . . .

PIMPLE: Did you hurt him, Paul? Did you knock him out?

SAFF: He's lying in an oxygen tent. Tubes up his nose.

PAUL (*screaming*): You might be right cunt! (*Quieter to* PIMPLE:) He went down, bleeding. Hit me first . . . whacked me with something. Bit dizzy like, headache. (*Pause.*) That's entertainment though innit – that's what it says on their new LP. Jam I mean.

SAFF: I told him he should go up the hospital. In the casualty.

PIMPLE: You should Paul.

PAUL: Can't go anywhere yet. They'll be looking for us. Me and Saff.

SAFF: Am I brown yet? Do I look Mediterranean or what?

PIMPLE: Sure it weren't you that got hit on the head?

PAUL: I bet the river has dried up, don't you?

SAFF: Pubs must be doing a good business.

PIMPLE: Everyone's got their front door open on our landing. You can see everyone's wallpaper. Don't like the bloody hot weather – makes the rubbish chute smell and all the rats come out . . . and there's only bloody boring cricket on the telly. Bloody hate summer.

SAFF: You got a friend here, Pimple. A mate. Paul here has just been saying what a wank summer is.

PAUL: In the city. In the city I said.

PIMPLE: And all I get at home is bloody salad. Bloody salad every night. I mean, I'm supposed to build meself up so I can take all the knocks. Fill out, like for when I get a trial. How can I take all the knocks eating bloody beetroot and lettuce all the time. It's stupid innit. I bet Brooking don't eat fucking salad.

SAFF: That all you reckon summer boils down to, Pimple – salads and stinking chutes? What about the long, warm evenings? The lazy Sunday afternoons. Strolls through the park, drinks by the pool.

PAUL: Picnics.

SAFF: Tea and scones.

PAUL: In the teashop.

SAFF: What about it all that?

PIMPLE: Well, that's a joke innit? A load of shit.

SAFF: That's what I like to hear Pimple. A bit of a thoughtful argument. I can see you made a careful study so's you could speak with authority like. And your conclusion is, your findings say . . .

PIMPLE: That it's all shit. All what you said about summer. All shit.

SAFF: That all they taught you at school, Pimple?

PIMPLE: Yeah, shit.

PAUL: You left now?

PIMPLE: Yeah, about six weeks ago. Waste of time doing exams. I been round the Jobcentre looking in the self-service.

PAUL: Like everyone else.

PIMPLE: Nothing. Wank. That's what I thought.

PAUL: Like everyone else.

PIMPLE: Can't even sign on yet. I was thinking – it's just as well I'm going to be snapped up for West Ham and England. (*Pause.*) They still had some of your drawings at school Paul. They was still on the wall. Brilliant – that one of the tramp. You must have been the best in your year at art. D'you still draw things?

PAUL: Yeah . . . don't show 'em to no-one though. People laugh . . . if they know you do things like that. Drawing.

SAFF: I can't do nothing except tell jokes and cash me giro. That ain't much good is it? Me old man reckons it's kids like me that give this area a bad name. Yeah I know, I says. We call it pisshole. Punches me in the chest don't he? No sense of humour that's his trouble. He says it's my fault me mum's on Valium. That ain't right, is it?

PAUL: I heard they've started putting Valium in the tap water – to keep us all quiet. Make us tame.

SAFF: Here – d'you hear about the old couple in my block – they thought someone was trying to break down the door and rob 'em – the old man put a table up against the door and the old woman got so frightened she had a stroke. Turns out it was meals on wheels come to pay a visit.

PIMPLE: Probably thought they was skinheads. I'm a skinhead but I ain't had me hair cut yet. I'm going to try and get a pair of Dr Martins for me birthday. Smart eh?

PAUL: You'll be the belle of the ball.

SAFF: A real tasty geezer.

PIMPLE: Well, if you're going to be a skin you got to have all the gear. British Movement innit?

SAFF: Hear that Paul, he's joined the professionals.

PAUL: He's all brave.

PIMPLE: Fuck off! Nar, leave it out. This bloke has been coming round the flats. He knows Chivers, see. From West Ham – he gives out leaflets there. He was saying about how we ain't a pure race no more, this country getting swamped by pakis and spades. He says this country has gone downhill ever since. He's right though ain't he. He give us a badge each with a Union Jack and a dragon on it. He says the blacks have got all the white people's jobs. We ought to make 'em sorry they ever come over here. Our duty, he reckons. The other night me and the others went round and smashed some pakis windows – it was right funny. We're all going to be in it proper now.

SAFF: Cor fuck me! We got an international terrorist with us. A mercenary on our hands, a dog of war and all that.

PIMPLE: This bloke, right . . .

SAFF: Here – how many passports you got? I bet Pimple ain't your real name is it? Oh you devil! I hope you ain't going to take us hostage. Urban guerrilla ain't he?

PAUL: Action man.

PIMPLE: So, it was a laugh.

PAUL: Yeah – how d'you think the pakis felt – and their kids?

SAFF: Bit fucking cold like – no windows.

PIMPLE: Pakis shouldn't have all the best housing anyway. Shouldn't have the same as us.

PAUL: What – like on our estate you mean? (*Pause.*) You're dumb, Pimple.

PIMPLE: Bloke says he might be able to pay us – that won't be dumb. And we're all out of work ain't we – look at all the coons that got jobs on London Transport. That's proof innit?

PAUL: Smashing their windows ain't going to change nothing. Give you kicks for a bit, that's all. Ain't going to stop the rubbish chutes stinking, ain't going to give you somewhere to go. You should tell him to stick his dragon and his Union Jack up his arse. We ain't got nothing to be patriotic about.

SAFF: What's a matter with you! (*To* PIMPLE:) D'you hear that! He's right

quiet usually ain't he – he don't say a word, keeps things to himself. (*Back again.*) Now the sun's gone to your head and you sound like a fucking social worker. All holy like.

PAUL: Don't tell me who I sound like! (*Quieter.*) It's suffocating me round here, it's smothering me! Streets of corrugated iron and hanging round waiting for something and broken bottles in the dark. All them families behind rows and rows of doors in the flats. Even their curtains are grey. Life sentence, right! They ain't got a choice – we ain't either. We're stuck here. Home innit! (*Quieter.*) I ain't no social worker.

SAFF: Bit of a speech Paul. Don't know why you talk like that. No wonder you're always going on about the Jam. But he only smashed a few pakis' windows.

PIMPLE: Everyone's a skin now anyway.

PAUL: Thought you was trying to get a trial.

SAFF: He smashed windows in his spare time. Sort of hobby. Ain't that right, Pimple?

PAUL: Head feels like it's been cracked like an egg.

SAFF: We might as well go now. (*Picking up his shirt.*)

PAUL (*shouts*): I can't go home!

SAFF: Why, in case they got a warrant? Watching your house? Smash the door down? (*To* PIMPLE:) How much d'you say he'd give you?

PIMPLE: He said it might be as much as a fiver – we gotta earn it though he says.

SAFF: What – for giving the pakis a bit of ventilation? No wonder they always got bandages round their heads – all of them bricks going through their windows. I love the sound of breaking glass.

PAUL: We could piss off somewhere Saff . . . me and you. We need to get away, need a change of place – that's Paul Weller's lyrics. Jam's a fucking great group.

PIMPLE: This bloke used to be in the Army. He says the British Movement put Britain first. Make Britain great again he reckons – join the British Movement. He says he might use us in a few weeks' time –

they're having a march through Dalston.
Join up proper like. A new future with
white power. Go on the march, like.
Better than nothing.

SAFF: Especially if you might get some
money.

PAUL: Saff, they'll kick me to pieces if they
find me. In the interview room – just them
and me. You got no chance if you hurt a
copper right?

SAFF (*to* PIMPLE): This bloke . . . will he
be about next week? You gotta sign any
forms?

PIMPLE: Nah – but when you go on a
march, you get this armband to wear.
And you might get a Union Jack to carry.

SAFF: I'll fly the flag if there's a fiver in it.
He might be conning you though.

PIMPLE: He comes round the flats. I'm
surprised you ain't seen him. Chivers got
him to come round . . . he stands outside
Upton Park. I'll be meeting him later on.

PAUL: If you wanna throw stones, Saff,
come down to Folkestone with us, yeah.
Walk along the beach, see for miles you
can. We could lie on the sand, stay for
ages – enjoying the sun. Can't enjoy
nothing round here. Place is grey – know
what I mean?

SAFF: You might as well be talking French.
(*He starts to go.*)

PIMPLE (*having retrieved his football, is
peering into a cardboard box*): Fucking
hell!

SAFF (*joining him*): What's the matter?
(*Pause.*) Shit!

PAUL: You're all dried up Saff. Paul
Weller says that in that song. You're
talking like some fucking hardened MP.

PIMPLE: Is it dead?

SAFF: I can't hear it breathing.

PAUL: Sometimes I wish I was Paul Weller.
I wish I could write songs like that. About
the lights and the pretty girls.

PIMPLE: It's all pink. Shall I pick it up?

SAFF: Go on then.

PAUL: What is it?

PIMPLE: What about fingerprints?

SAFF: Wanker! Go on.

PAUL: What you looking at?

SAFF: Come and have a look. You ain't
gonna fucking believe it.

PIMPLE: What if it's dead.

SAFF: Then you won't wake it up will ya?

PIMPLE: It's been abandoned.

SAFF: Course it fucking has.

PAUL: A baby!

PIMPLE: How can you tell if it's a boy or a
girl?

SAFF: How d'you think?

PAUL: You're joking!

SAFF (*to* PAUL): Sssh! You'll wake it up.

PAUL: Left here? Jesus.

SAFF: Have a butchers. It's not dead. It's
only little.

As PAUL *bends over,* SAFF *pulls in and
throws it at* PAUL. *It is a doll.* SAFF *and*
PIMPLE *break up with laughter.*

SAFF: April fool!

PIMPLE: Cindy doll! All squeaky.

PAUL: Cunts.

SAFF: Had you going.

PAUL: Stupid.

SAFF: I really thought it was a real one at
first.

PIMPLE: Me an all.

PAUL: Wouldn't have mattered to you if it
was. (*Holding the doll up to* SAFF.)

SAFF: Nah – I suppose you're right. Might
have got a reward if it'd been a real one.

PAUL: Nothing touches you does it?

SAFF (*pushing the doll out of* PAUL's
hands): Blame it on me environment.

PIMPLE: We was only having a laugh.

PAUL: Keep out of this cunt!

SAFF: It's all right Pimple. Paul can't take a
joke. Takes everything to heart Paul
does. He's got feelings.

PAUL: You got no fucking feelings.

SAFF: That right? You an expert eh? Listen
cunt – I used to want things – wanted a
job, wanted flash gear, I even wanted to
play at Hammersmith Odeon once, Jam

fan. Me own band an all that. When Mick got done for smashing that school up – he wanted things – and he got put away. I used to have all these daydreams about how things would turn out. People used to laugh at me, take the piss – when I said. Now I laugh at them – I like it better that way round. So now I don't ask for nothing and I don't expect nothing. I just wake up in the mornings and everything else is a joke. I've given up all that wanting shit. Terrible thing innit? You'll find out the same thing, poet.

PAUL: Don't fucking tell me. I've found out enough.

SAFF: Still wanna have a day trip to Folkestone – get away from it all?

PAUL: Vegetable – you ain't alive.

PIMPLE: It was only a joke. It was only a doll for fuck's sake.

SAFF: I don't reckon Paul likes living around here – it's too hard for him. Going on about the Old Bill like it had never happened to anyone else. (*To* PAUL:) You'd be better off drawing pictures in your bedroom, listening to your records.

PAUL: Waste of time listening to you.

SAFF: Hard game innit – being a thief?

PAUL: Only thing you can do – and you can't even do that properly.

SAFF: Weren't me that got the dig from the copper.

PAUL: I was trying to get away, right. Pity he didn't hit you instead.

SAFF (*running to where the briefcase is hidden*): We nicked a geezer's case just before, Pimple – out his car. Flash motor – Jag. He must have been worth a few bob – and where that bloke comes from – from some fucking crescent or avenue in Rainham with his double glazing and his lawns and his sons doing them Duke of Edinburgh awards, and all the family going for a walk after Sunday dinner – that's what old Paul here wants, he wants to live there. You heard him before didn't ya? It's too grey for him round him. Ain't that right Paul?

PIMPLE: Look, I don't know what this is all about. I only came over here to find somewhere to . . .

PAUL *grabs a piece of wood.*

PAUL (*to* SAFF): You fucking liar! Come on then!

PIMPLE: Leave it out Paul. Let's go back to the flats. Let's go home, yeah.

PAUL: We ain't going nowhere are we?

SAFF: No we ain't.

PIMPLE: I gotta go off to meet that bloke. He's got some leaflets for us to put through the door. Facts and figures about the blacks!

PAUL: Don't you move!

SAFF (*sarcastic*): Police are searching the area.

PIMPLE: He says the British public are at the end of their tether. The whole country is burning a slow fuse. It's going to explode soon!

PAUL: Throbbing – like me brains shaking.

SAFF: Excuses now eh – wanna bottle out?

PIMPLE: All the muggings the blacks do. Everything'll be all right when we get the spades and the Jews out. Be a better life for all of us. A new future to look forward to for a change. New future with white power! Skinhead warriors!

PAUL: Fucking take your shirt off you!

PIMPLE: What?

SAFF: He's a lunatic. He's got more than delayed concussion or whatever they call it.

PAUL: You heard! Take it off! And your trousers!

PIMPLE (*as he strips*): What you going to do!

PAUL: That's it – let the sun get at you! In your pores! Fresh air – good for you! Colour in your cheeks. Lovely weather for it!

PIMPLE: I feel stupid like this. You wait you bastard. Me cousins . . .

PAUL: Stop talking! Can't concentrate . . . it's funny, like being drunk . . . Everything's going round really fast . . . dizzy. Cunt copper . . . law and order . . .

SAFF *goes for* PAUL. *They fight violently.* PAUL *bangs* SAFF's *head against the fence.* SAFF *goes down.* PIMPLE *is still standing there in his pants.*

Pause. PAUL *begins to talk to* SAFF *who is writhing in pain on the floor, clutching his head.*

Be coming over on the police radio about us Saff . . . clever dick codewords. We gotta get away – Folkestone, right. Be great. It's too grey here. In the interview room – just them and me. Sorry Saff, sorry. Think I'll put me shirt back on. Paul Weller – great songs . . . I'd like to write them songs. It hurts Saff. It hurts.

Lights dim.

DEALT WITH

Dealt With was first presented as part of a double bill with its companion play, *London Calling*, at the Theatre Royal, Stratford E15, on 13 November 1981, with the following cast:

PIMPLE	Martin Murphy
SAFF	John Folwer
ROY	Victor Romero Evans
PAUL	Jamie Foreman
BENDALL	David Allister

Directed by Adrian Shergold
Decor by Jenny Tiramani
Lighting by Gerry Jenkinson
Sound by Simon Curry

Scene One

PIMPLE *is painting a wall, slowly and with boredom. He continues for a few moments then stops and looks to see if anyone is watching. He starts to paint 'WOGS OUT' on the wall. He stands back, looks at it. A voice calls him. He looks round sharply, a bit nervous. He is called again. He sees SAFF, on top of the wall.*

PIMPLE: Fuck me!

SAFF *jumps down.*

PIMPLE (*goes over, off*): All right mate! I didn't know you was coming home! Over here.

SAFF *is wearing borstal uniform and is looking round, a bit wary, edgy as PIMPLE talks to him.*

It's all right, I'm on me own. I'm the only one here. How d'you know I was working on this scheme then?

SAFF: Phoned your house.

PIMPLE: When d'you get out – today? Must be right pleased. Nice to be out, eh?

SAFF: I done a bunk, Pimple.

PIMPLE (*disbelieving*): Yeah I reckon – and I'm Prince Charles if you have.

SAFF: What do you think this is then – fancy dress? (*Silence for a moment, PIMPLE is thinking about it.*) I ain't joking!

PIMPLE: You ain't are you!

SAFF: All right Your Royal Highness.

PIMPLE: What – you run away, pissed off without 'em knowing! Over the wall, like? Fucking hell – must have took some doing. A lot of bottle to do that eh! How d'you get down here?

SAFF: In a car.

PIMPLE: What – hitch-hiking!

SAFF: Not exactly.

PIMPLE: Nicked a car as well! Pothouse you are! But I didn't know you could drive.

SAFF: I can't.

PIMPLE: Then how . . .

SAFF: Brought someone with me. Mate from Slough. (*He calls.*) Roy!

ROY *comes over the top of the wall. He is black.*

ROY (*to* PIMPLE): All right.

PIMPLE (*looking quickly at the* 'WOGS OUT'): Oh . . . hello . . . all right . . . how you doing? My name's Pimple. (*He holds out his hand. He looks again at the graffiti.*) So the two of you done a bunk then? (*He subsequently tries to hide the writing with his body.*)

SAFF: Sherlock Holmes ain't he?

PIMPLE: You been home yet?

SAFF: Can't. That's the last place I can go.

PIMPLE: Why's that?

SAFF: Cos it's the first place they'll look. You seen Paul? Lately I mean.

PIMPLE: Yeah, he's supposed to be coming round here at dinner-time as it happens – when I'm on me lunch break. I got some old LPs of me dad's to lend him. He wanted to hear 'em. Kinks and Tamla Motown stuff. He's getting into all that sixties gear now. He's coming round to pick 'em up – they're down there. He was right interested when I told him . . .

SAFF (*interrupting*): Dinner-time you said. What time's dinner-time?

PIMPLE: About half-one.

ROY: It's about quarter past now.

SAFF: And he's definitely coming?

PIMPLE: So he said. If he don't, then I gotta carry all the LPs back home again ain't I?

SAFF: We'll wait here for him then. Is anyone else going to show up? Anyone you work for like.

PIMPLE: Nah, they leave me on me own most of the time. I'm one of them experience schemes – working for this firm. (*Pause.*) Is Paul going to help you then?

SAFF: I hope.

PIMPLE: Did he know you was going to have it away? Did you tell him when he come to visit?

SAFF: Didn't start thinking about it till last week.

ROY: So what you doing on the scheme then?

PIMPLE: Me careers officer told me about it. This all that there is, he said. Jobcentre sent me here – they got posters up saying it was like throwing a lifebuoy to a drowning man. And breaking the vicious circle. They said what I needed was experience of the working world. They said I needed an opportunity. So here I am.

ROY: What d'you do then?

PIMPLE: At the moment I'm learning how to paint walls. Getting training like. (*Leaning against the wall in an attempt to hide the writing and gets paint on his hands.*) I'm being given the chance to become sort of qualified in painting walls. At the end of it all, I'm going to get a certificate – to say I've got experience.

SAFF: Experience of what?

PIMPLE: Well, painting walls for a start. Yeah, this certificate is going to prove I've been trained in things.

SAFF: You'll be a fully qualified painter.

PIMPLE: I'm supposed to be learning how to work a forklift – so the Jobcentre said anyway. Ain't happened yet though. Bloke says I ain't ready for it. Be smart when it happens, when I do. Last two months, I just been sweeping up in the yard and breaking up tea chests.

SAFF: Bit of a wank innit?

PIMPLE: It is when I have to clean the bloke's car and run round the shops to get sandwiches for everybody. Jobcentre didn't say I'd be doing that when I came here. I'm supposed to be here for six months altogether.

SAFF: What happens after that?

PIMPLE: I dunno really. Banksy went on one of these schemes and at the end of it they just said to him, 'Thanks a lot – good luck in the future'. Then he went back on the dole. If that happens to me, then all that stuff they got in the Jobcentre about saving a drowning man and breaking the vicious circle – all be lies won't it?

SAFF: What about your certificate?

PIMPLE: Oh yeah. I suppose I can take it round all the firms when I go for jobs. Impress 'em like – with all the experience it says I've got. They'll know they're getting someone who's trained up.

Probably won't ever get to have a go of the forklift so it won't mention that.

SAFF: Must be a lot of other kids with these certificates, who've been on these schemes.

ROY: About four hundred thousand.

SAFF: How comes you know so much about it?

ROY: I been on three schemes since I left school. I've got a veterans medal. (*To* PIMPLE:) They still paying £23 a week?

PIMPLE: Yeah.

SAFF: Oh – so it's part time then?

PIMPLE: No – half nine till half five. It's a full working week, like in the working world. What I need is a longer lunch hour.

SAFF: What you need is Arthur fucking Scargill. (*Pause.*) Must be about half past now. You sure he said half past?

PIMPLE: Positive – that's when me dinner-time starts.

ROY: Who done that? (*Noticing the graffiti.*)

PIMPLE: What . . . oh that. Yeah, I noticed that. I was just going to paint it off as part of my training. Cover it up like. Instructions from the bloke – cover up any graffiti. That's graffiti innit? Skinheads I reckon – breaking in and using this paint. It's bad if you ask me. I mean, I like blacks. You're black ain't ya?

PAUL *enters. He is wearing a suit.*

SAFF: All right Paul – been waiting for you.

PAUL: Jesus Saff – I didn't know you was home.

SAFF: It's a bit of a secret.

PAUL: What d'you mean? What you doing here? You been looking for me?

SAFF: Yeah – you pleased to see me?

PAUL: Course – bit of a surprise that's all.

SAFF: It was a bit unexpected. Didn't know till the last minute.

PAUL: Bit unusual innit? What did your old man say?

SAFF: I ain't seen him yet.

PAUL: What about your mum?

SAFF: No. Her neither. (*Pause.*)

PAUL: I don't understand – d'you get out today?

SAFF: This morning. But I shouldn't have.

PAUL: Shouldn't have what?

SAFF: I come down in someone's Anglia.

PAUL: What you saying? You got a lift?

SAFF: What d'you think I'm saying?

PAUL: You done a bunk? You gotta be joking!

SAFF: Well, I ain't exactly bought an Awayday ticket for fuck's sake.

PAUL: You never said nothing when I came to Slough.

SAFF: Hard to talk then. You only say little things, what's on the surface, like – especially with the screws there. This is Roy. This is Paul.

PAUL: Hello, all right.

ROY: All right, how you doing?

PAUL: Why you done it, Saff?

SAFF: Just had to.

PAUL: Have either of you thought where you're going to go or what you're going to do?

SAFF: Not a lot.

PAUL: You're fucking mad. Have you had anything to eat?

SAFF: Roy said he could eat a horse so we went in a Wimpy Bar. (*They laugh, except* PIMPLE.)

PIMPLE: I don't get it. (*Pause.*)

ROY (*to* PIMPLE): You wouldn't have any sandwiches going spare would ya?

PIMPLE: Cheese and pickle any good?

ROY: Luxury.

SAFF: We need a few favours Paul. That's why we been waiting for you.

PAUL: Somewhere to stay.

SAFF: If it don't mean a lot of aggravation for you. And change of clothes. A bit quick, like.

PAUL: That's no problem.

SAFF: Money is though. We've got about seventy-five pence between us.

ROY: Any salt?

PIMPLE: Got some plain crisps. Plenty of salt in them.

ROY: You're a brother.

PIMPLE: No, Golden Wonder.

ROY: Sorry?

PAUL: How much you got on ya Pimple?

PIMPLE: Just a packet of cheese and onion.

PAUL: No, money I mean. (*To* SAFF:) Me mum's got something in her savings book.

SAFF: Don't be silly.

PIMPLE: There might be something on the telly – about you two!

SAFF: Be surprised if we make page fourteen of the *Daily Mirror*.

PIMPLE: Must be a great feeling – being on the run.

ROY: Helter skelter.

PIMPLE: Eh?

ROY: That's what it's like. Going hundred miles an hour down an helter skelter.

PIMPLE: Without a mat sort of thing.

They all look at him.

PAUL: Thought you might have gone somewhere else – instead of coming back here.

SAFF: Seemed the only thing to do. Anyway, it's all I know innit? (*Pause.*) Got to get hold of some money Paul – or we're fucked. Like having diarrhoea and no toilet paper.

PAUL: I'm trying to think of something.

ROY: We could go across London . . . see me brother in Brixton. He might be able to score some cash for us.

SAFF: What if he can't?

ROY: Be nice to see him anyway.

PAUL: What d'you think there might be in an office Saff?

SAFF: What d'you mean?

PAUL: Well, like stuff to nick.

SAFF: A desk and two chairs.

PAUL: You know what I mean.

SAFF: Petty cash box. Calculators. Might find some money left in drawers.

ROY: Might be a little safe – for valuables, like. Depends What sort of office,

SAFF: Pound notes in jars for the tea club.

PIMPLE: A clock on the wall. (*They look at him.*)

PAUL: A fat wallet in a jacket pocket.

SAFF: What you thinking about?

PAUL: Helping you out.

SAFF: You're making my mouth water. Where's all this at?

PAUL: Bound to be something like that there.

SAFF: Where for fuck's sake.

PAUL: Where I been . . . this morning. Interview. Where I got shit on but couldn't smell nothing – cos it's all done with smiles and hints.

SAFF: And we might be lucky if we go there? Get a result like?

PAUL: You won't go away with nothing, I know it. Pay a return visit to that superior bastard. Thinks he won't have to bother with me again. Just another loser.

SAFF: What d'you reckon Roy – go there or not?

ROY: We gotta take some chances or else we won't be going nowhere except back to Slough.

SAFF: Don't sound like a soft touch.

ROY: No choice.

SAFF: How we going to handle the geezer?

PAUL: I'll occupy him.

SAFF: I don't understand what you're going to get out of this, Paul.

PAUL: I've got to be given me life back, y'know starting today, starting this afternoon. Can't keep accepting.

SAFF *and* ROY *look at each other.*

SAFF: Whatever you say, Paul. As long as we end up with something in our pockets.

PIMPLE: D'you want any help?

SAFF: Has this geezer got a secretary? In the office next door or something?

PAUL: No, he's on his own. Won't be on his own this afternoon, though. Come back to my house first and change your gear. Me mum's at work.

PIMPLE: What about the LPs, Paul?

PAUL: You brought 'em?

PIMPLE: They're down there.

PAUL: Thanks. Grateful to you.

PIMPLE: Let us come with you, yeah. I'm resigning. I'm jacking it in. It's a fucking rip-off if you ask me. I've decided I ain't going to put up with it no more. They can stick it up their arse. I'm with you three.

ROY: Raring to go then.

SAFF: You're sure about this, Paul?

PAUL: I don't feel like I got nothing to lose any more.

SAFF: I know what you mean. That's how I felt when I was climbing over the wall.

PAUL: Coming then?

PAUL, ROY *and* SAFF *on the way out.* PIMPLE *picks up the paint and brushes.*

SAFF (*to* PIMPLE): Hurry up then. (SAFF *goes.*)

PIMPLE: Wait for us will ya! (*He puts the brush down.*) You forgot the LPs, Paul. (*He picks them up, carrying them offstage.*) Paul – what about the LPs?

Crash in with 'Eton Rifles'.

Scene Two

An office. BENDALL *is working at the desk. The door opens.* PAUL *enters.*

BENDALL: What the hell! Who are you?

PAUL: Paul.

BENDALL: Ever heard of knocking? Can I help you?

PAUL: Yeah, you can help.

BENDALL (*angry*): Look – what is this!

PAUL: I've come to see if you've changed your mind. About me, like. I saw you this morning.

BENDALL: The vacancy for stockroom assistant . . . yes, I recall your face. And you've come back for what?

PAUL: See if you've changed your mind. You rang the Jobcentre to tell 'em you didn't want me.

BENDALL: If you think this is some kind of joke, you'd better find a better audience – I don't think I understand. How did you get past our security man?

PAUL: I made meself invisible.

BENDALL: Well, I think you'd better manage that trick again don't you . . . through that door, the one you just found with your foot. After all, I'm sure that your invisibility is by far your most attractive feature.

PAUL: I thought if I came back and saw you . . . asked for another chance, you might think again like.

BENDALL: If all the people I saw decided to turn up here asking for another chance . . .

PAUL: Then you'd have a very long queue.

BENDALL: Very good.

PAUL: I'm trying.

BENDALL: Yes you are, very trying. Get out now please.

PAUL: So you won't change your mind?

BENDALL: Unscrambled the code at last, have you? Now, having untangled the intricacies of one sentence, here's another: piss off sonny.

PAUL: Not even a little bit, not by the hairs of your chinny chin chin.

BENDALL: Someone is going to come through that door any moment – will you be running off then or before?

PAUL: You got a sign up outside that says please knock. On the other side it says Meeting in Progress. That's what this is. So we won't be disturbed, see.

BENDALL: Who do you think you are, some kind of little gangster? James Cagney or Napoleon? Come on, which is it, eh? A touch of bravado maybe, a 'dare' from your 'mates'? Or is it just stupidity?

PAUL: I've got a lot of choices ain't I? What d'you think I should pick?

BENDALL: If you're capable of having any sort of thoughts, I'd be having second ones right now about being here at all. I'm very near to losing my temper.

PAUL: See this suit – this is what I had on this morning – d'you remember? It was me dad's. First time it's been worn. Since he died, like. It's a Burtons off the peg. Smells a bit musty – been in the wardrobe for ages. But nice cut. Small lapels – all the rage now. Seven inch wide trouser bottoms. It's the gear. Mod innit? Mod gear. My dad would have laughed if he'd known how tasty he was. How fashionable like. Mind you, can't imagine him jumping up and down to the Jam though. That's what all the kids wear when they go and see the Jam – suits like this.

BENDALL: Last warning – before I call the security guard. (*Picking up the phone.*)

PAUL (*sitting down*): What – phone him up you mean?

BENDALL: No, I'll beat out a bloody message on the tom-toms. (*Dialling. Pause.*) Joe – it's John Bendall here. Can you come down here right away? Some young joker in my office . . . thinks he's a gangster. Sorry? Yes, quite uninvited. No, I don't know how he got in – over the wall presumably. Yes, OK . . . see you in a minute. (*He puts the phone down.*) Satisfied?

PAUL: Very businesslike that was.

BENDALL: I was hoping you'd appreciate it. Very shortly, a rather well-built man in a black uniform will be performing here live and the lapels of your fashionable jacket are going to get very creased – when he picks you up by them.

PAUL: It's a Burtons off the peg.

BENDALL: I'm at a loss trying to understand what you were hoping to achieve. It's not April, so it can't be April fool – unless you've got a 364 day extension – to make it a permanent feature in your life. The professional fool. Obviously though, you understand that you were unsuccessful this morning – but you turn up here attempting I don't know what. The police can already arrest you for trespass even if they don't catch you here. You seem to have forgotten that your name and address are on our files – it would be a very simple matter for them to find you. And if you haven't realised that, then it's just as well I didn't take you on. We might have knaves working for us – but we don't have fools. Which brings us back to square one.

PAUL: That was very convincing – that conversation you had on the phone.

BENDALL (*loudly*): When he comes you'll find yourself leaving here with a red face and a black and blue arse.

PAUL: He weren't there.

BENDALL: We'll see.

PAUL: I know. He's in the betting shop. I saw him walk over there. That's why you didn't get any answer just now. When he walked into the betting shop, I walked through the gates. You can't get the staff these days can you? Always skiving.

BENDALL: OK! I think this has gone far enough, don't you? A court appearance won't be nearly so funny as you seem to think this is. You'd better save your quaint sense of humour for the police.

PAUL: You seem a bit cross. A bit upset like.

BENDALL: Fine – you stay here. Take my seat if you like – there's some correspondence there you might like to deal with. I'll go and find someone or I'll bloody well move you myself if I have to. (*Getting up.*)

PAUL: I want you to stay here – listen to me.

BENDALL: Listen to you? I think I've heard enough. Think I've seen enough. (*Going out.*)

PAUL (*screaming*): Listen to me I said!

BENDALL: Stick it, chum. (*Going to the door.*)

PAUL (*quieter*): Mates are out there. They'll stop you.

BENDALL: Of course they are. Don't tell me – there's a whole gang of them. It's a guerrilla attack. The East London freedom fighters, affiliated to the TUC. Earlier you referred to I not we. I'm not stupid, but I am going to have you removed. (*He opens the door and encounters* SAFF *and* ROY.) Jesus Christ.

SAFF: That's the nicest thing anyone has ever said to me. Hello, we're the heavies.

ROY: I'm heavier than him.

PAUL: Told you.

BENDALL: I won't be intimidated. D'you hear? Look, response to the job was phenomenal . . . I've been seeing people for the last three days. I compiled a shortlist and from that I made a choice. You weren't it I'm afraid. You'll just have to understand that.

PAUL: You laughed at me.

BENDALL: What?

PAUL: Don't get a chance for many interviews see. Not an expert or nothing. Round here – no jobs to have interviews for. Every time I do get one – it's the same answer. Jobs like this bobbing up and down in an ocean of nothing . . . like a life raft. Something to try and cling onto, but I get a foot on me head pushing me away. Yours this time.

SAFF: Paul's my mate. You upset him.

ROY: Hurt his feelings like.

SAFF: Dashed his hopes you did.

BENDALL: I am not here to justify anything to you. Certainly not under these circumstances, not to you characters.

PAUL: I got up at six o'clock this morning. Went round the paper shop, bought all the newspapers. The good ones. Guardian, Daily Telegraph. All them. I was reading them for news, see.

BENDALL: Well well – we live and learn, don't we?

PAUL: Getting information, general knowledge and that. Show an interest in current affairs, what was happening in the world. So's I could talk about it, like. If you asked me stuff.

BENDALL: You were being interviewed for the job of stockroom assistant. You were not being asked to make an appearance on University Challenge.

PAUL: I know, yeah – but I tried . . . I thought I'd try . . . to make an impression. Impress you – and you'd take me on. But . . .

SAFF: But you weren't having none of it. And now look what's happened.

BENDALL: I take it you're the comedian, the joker in the pack.

SAFF: That's right – and this is the ace of spades.

ROY: He reminds me of Wilcox and Sulley. At Slough. That way they got of talking to you, you know what I mean. Like you was a piece of shit that had got onto their shoe. A piece of shit they was scraping off by the kerb.

BENDALL: How do you expect me to react – by opening a bottle of champagne?

PAUL: We could do the interview again. Might be different this time.

SAFF: Come on Roy. Let's do the business.

SAFF *and* ROY *begin to look for money etc. in drawers and cabinets.*

BENDALL: You've got some kind of nerve! What do you think you're looking for?

SAFF: It's all right mister – we're just spring cleaning.

BENDALL: Robbery added to trespassing. What next? A touch of arson to complete a set? (*To* PAUL:) For Christ's sake – I'm warning you. There'll be bloody dire consequences for this.

SAFF: We know all about consequences. We've spent months learning about consequences from a place run by geezers like you. Consequences means swapping fags for a dirty book, calling the sadistic bastards there sir and not screwing anyone during dinner in case they put their knife and fork in your back. We had enough of consequences, all right. (*To* ROY:) Anything?

ROY (*pulling out various items of stationery, from* BENDALL's *desk, like scissors, rubbers, envelopes, paper, and saying the following correspondingly*): Yeah – emeralds, diamonds, twenty pound notes, gold bars and the fucking Holy Grail. And a packet of drawing pins.

SAFF: Keep the drawing pins – all the other stuff is shit. (*He picks up the phone.*)

BENDALL: Keep away from there! There's nothing in there of any value . . . you won't find anything.

SAFF (*producing a broken bottle*): I hope you ain't going to be a nuisance.

BENDALL *moves away as* SAFF *goes through the desk.*

BENDALL: This is stupid . . . pointless . . .

there's nothing to steal. (*Pause.*) Throwing petrol bombs at the police gets boring does it?

SAFF: Yeah – this breaks the fucking monotony for us. There's something missing here.

BENDALL: Your charm and grace I would have thought.

ROY: What d'you mean – something missing?

SAFF: Well, geezers like him who have desks. They usually have pictures of their wife. On the desk like. Smiling (*To* BENDALL:) Why ain't you got a picture of her?

ROY: Is she ugly mister? Would she put me off me dinner?

SAFF: Bit of a dog? Would a picture of her spoil the desk. (*To* ROY:) I bet he calls her dear. I bet they do it with the light out and a tea-towel under her bum.

ROY: It's not nice is it – stains on the sheets?

BENDALL: I can see we're into Noël Coward territory now.

SAFF: Nice conversation we're having.

BENDALL: The level of conversation wouldn't do credit to a garden slug.

SAFF: Nothing so far Paul. Wash-out.

PAUL: What about him.

SAFF: Has to be. (*To* BENDALL:) Ain't your day is it? – Empty your pockets out.

BENDALL: No way. No way at all. I refuse. Absolutely.

SAFF (*indicating the broken bottle to* BENDALL): We didn't come here to hurt you, but we can arrange it, all right. How would you like your guts emptied out on the floor like a tin of spaghetti? I've been called lots of names in the past few months – like slag, scum, moronic cunt, animal, savage, barbarian. Every day, hearing them names you start to believe 'em, that what they're calling you is right. See, at the moment I ain't supposed to be fit to walk the streets and an animal like me, if that's what I am, wouldn't give a fuck about hurting you. (*He shouts.*) Pockets!!

BENDALL (*reaching for his wallet and throwing it on the desk*): One wallet.

ROY (*picks it up and thumbs through it*): He's got a Barclaycard! (*To* BENDALL:) I think I'd prefer American Express – they've got unlimited credit ain't they. Yeah, I'd like a bit of plastic. Don't like to carry too much cash about with me. Can't be too careful nowadays – never know who might be lurking about. Yeah, one day I'm going to have me own set of credit cards. (*He throws it to* SAFF.)

SAFF (*counting*): Forty quid and some change.

PAUL: Is it enough?

SAFF: It's bread and butter money. Means we can go somewhere. Live for a couple of days, till . . .

BENDALL: What do you hope to gain by doing this?

SAFF: Forty quid and credit cards.

PAUL: You got anything else? Like petty cash box or something, a safe . . .

BENDALL: You care about nothing, respect . . . nothing. Your lives . . . you seem bent on taking a depressing route nowhere . . . and in ugliness. Worse than that, you want to make other people's lives unpleasant. And you don't even know why. I really do feel sorry for you, all three of you.

SAFF: There's another one outside. You can feel sorry for him as well if you like.

PAUL: I was asking if you had anything else.

BENDALL (*shouting*): There's nothing. You can have my bloody luncheon vouchers if you like! And my shoelaces as well while you're at it! (*Taking the LVs out of his jacket pocket.*)

SAFF: Oh we've hit the jackpot! Luncheon Vouchers! We're having chicken! (*To* BENDALL:) I'm surprised you didn't have a barbed wire fence to protect these. I thought you might have hired Securicor or something. I bet you get all choked up when you have to hand them over in the sandwich bar.

BENDALL: Well, you keep them now – spoils of war.

SAFF: Who said anything about war?

BENDALL: I thought you and your friend had come here to declare it.

ROY: It's funny innit – borstal boys taking some office guy's luncheon vouchers.

PAUL: It's like a revolution innit?

BENDALL: Is that what's on your mind – your own private revolution.

SAFF: He ain't come for your credit cards.

BENDALL (*a bit worried, tense*): Hasn't this gone far enough . . . you've threatened me, you've taken my money . . . what else is there left for Christ's sake? You've evidently got what you wanted – why aren't you leaving? The longer you stay . . . the . . . the more likely it is you'll be caught. Only be a matter of time.

SAFF: Up to you, Paul – whatever you say.

PAUL: Don't wanna go yet. Ain't finished . . . yet.

BENDALL: Finished . . . finished what? Mark my words, when the law's finished with you, bloody future is going to be dim, very dim! No employer in the country would touch you with a disinfected bargepole. It won't just be me!

PAUL: Future's so dim already, I can't fucking see beyond tomorrow hardly. (*To* SAFF:) D'you mind Saff – just staying a bit?

SAFF: You've done us three favours – we ain't done you one yet.

PAUL: Thick as thieves, eh?

SAFF: What d'you mean?

PAUL: Don't matter.

BENDALL *has attempted to move very quickly to the door.*

ROY: Saff!

SAFF *goes for* BENDALL, *quickly followed by* ROY.

SAFF: It ain't going home time yet!

ROY: Tricky dicky.

BENDALL: Ah . . . all right . . . OK.

SAFF: We ain't finished our meeting yet!

BENDALL: Ah . . . I'm in no . . . no position to argue . . . tell them to lay off me will you . . .

SAFF: No action replays?

BENDALL: I've given you my assurance!

SAFF: Your assurance don't mean fuck all to me mate!

BENDALL: Let go! My enthusiasm for being a hero has diminished very suddenly. Honestly!

PAUL: All right Saff. Let go.

BENDALL: Your kindness is overwhelming.

PAUL: Ta.

BENDALL: I hope you're enjoying your new found position of power – it won't last. Never had it before have you? And will never have it again.

PAUL: All I know is you're not stirring your coffee now, not rubbing your chin with fucking boredom now. Power – that's what you had this morning.

BENDALL: So the real reason you've come back is to parade the old cliché about resentment of the figure of authority, which I take to be me in this case. Because I make decisions and sit behind a desk. Debunk and demystify yours truly and you'll feel a lot better – is that it? A little victory for a change? Well I'll tell you – by exhibiting your violence you'll change nothing sonny – you'll win nothing.

PAUL: When you started giving me all the details I thought you was mapping it out for me. When you started telling me about the social club and the squash court, the pension scheme and the holiday entitlements, the hours and the Christmas bonus – I thought I'm away here, he must want me if he's giving me all this – the big sell. That's what it sounded like. Other interviews never said fuck all like that. (*Pause.*) Bit embarrassed like . . . when you laughed about me reasons for wanting the job, bit disappointed like when you kept mentioning how many others you'd seen (*Screams.*). Bit fucking crushed when you didn't even ask to see me references! Well, here they are – read 'em . . . go on . . . read 'em. (*He thrusts the envelope in* BENDALL's *face. Quietly:*) Never had the chance to use 'em before. Things don't usually get that far. Nice things written down, all about me. Me art teacher at school – he done it for me.

BENDALL: And you seriously want me to read them?

PAUL: Out loud please.

SAFF (*with the broken bottle*): Go on, you've got a lovely voice, just like a newsreader. We want to hear it.

BENDALL (*opening the envelope, reading slowly, reluctantly at first. Should be painful and slightly embarrassing*): Since . . . knowing Paul . . . I have found him to be . . . an intelligent, sympathetic person . . . who makes an effort to get on well with other people. While not being particularly academic he is imaginative and hard-working and when required to work on a specific project . . . (*Breaking off.*) I'm afraid I don't see the relevance of all this. For whose benefit . . .

PAUL (*shouts*): Finish it! (*Softly.*) I like it. Make up for this morning.

BENDALL (*staring at* PAUL *for a few moments*): . . . during the lesson and at home he has done so conscientiously and with enthusiasm. One of Paul's qualities is his awareness of his own shortcomings and his wish to overcome them. It is a tendency that sometimes comes close to excessive self-criticism, but his conscientiousness has made him a trustworthy, reliable person always anxious to better himself.

PAUL (*taking the letter back, putting it in envelope*): Mr Roseberry. He done 'em for me. He believed in me, see. Thought I had something to offer. No one else had ever had any time for me, any interest. Two years I've had that. Been waiting for the chance to use it.

SAFF: Really his mum wrote all that.

BENDALL: In two years . . . adjectives can become out of date. It strikes me that some amendments might need making.

PAUL: If you'd read them this morning . . . I could be starting here Monday. I'm still available though. So what about it, then?

BENDALL: I'm not sure the chap who was successful would appreciate your . . . proposition.

PAUL: You don't know what it's like.

SAFF: Don't say that. He's got a hard life. Ain't you Mr Bendall. All that commuting he has to do. (*To*

BENDALL:) Must be terrible having to wait for the train every morning, holding your heavy briefcase. Especially when the trains don't come. Staff shortages, snow on the tracks. I bet you feel like throwing yourself under the cancellation board sometimes, don't ya?

ROY: I bet when he gets home after a hard day's work he has a sherry – to relax him like.

BENDALL: Dry Martini actually. Lemonade and plenty of ice.

SAFF: D'you do the crossword on the way home, does your wife meet you in the car?

ROY: You got a Volvo or a Rover?

SAFF: Bank manager call you by your first name does he?

ROY: He's got the Abbey habit.

BENDALL: Halifax. Impressive, isn't it?

SAFF: Don't tell me – you've got a formica kitchen and special jars for putting tea and coffee in. And fucking spices. What sort of music you into – James Last and his orchestra or James Galway and his magic flute? You got any kids?

Pause. BENDALL *refuses to respond. Silence.*

ROY: He don't wanna play this game.

SAFF: He's sulking.

BENDALL: Amazingly, I managed to keep my dick up long enough to have a son. He's six. You and he have a lot in common. Sense of humour and so on. But unlike you, he spends his days constructively, like learning to tie his shoes and spell words beginning with B. Like bat. Perhaps you never got to that stage. It would explain a lot.

ROY: Do you take him to the park to fly his model aeroplane.

SAFF: I bet you're one of them blokes who's always playing with his son's toys and you shout at him if he asks for 'em back. I bet you keep having a go of his model aeroplane and when the poor little fucker runs home crying, you run after him saying, 'Don't tell mummy, don't tell mummy'. I suppose you have to take him to the cubs every Monday and Friday. (*Pause.*) See Paul, he has got it rough, ain't he? What with greenfly in the rose bushes.

ROY: And fitting his sandwiches in the tupperware box every morning. You ain't got any by the way have you – sandwiches, like.

SAFF: Planning his holiday in Venice, arranging a squash match at his local club.

ROY: Creosoting the path.

SAFF: Folding the *Daily Telegraph*.

ROY: Tuning in to Radio 4.

SAFF: It's all fucking go innit? I'm surprised you don't have a nervous breakdown.

BENDALL: Name of the game is bait me, right? Watch me lose my cool, see the veins sticking out in my head. Wouldn't that be fun? The pay off. Well, no way I'm afraid. I refuse to recognise your crude attempt at a kangaroo court, your sneering cross-examination and what you imagine to be my lifestyle held up as some kind of evidence. Irony is, given the opportunity you'd drool all over the home I own and the car I drive. But you see, they didn't come free out of a packet of cornflakes. No one gave me anything. I worked.

PAUL: Yeah.

BENDALL: Sweated. From grammar school to evening classes I made a conscious effort to get somewhere, prove myself, and make bloody good use of what God gave me. I suppose you think that sounds corny eh? Pompous bit of back slapping? But think about this – I shall be here again tomorrow same as usual, sipping my coffee and using my calculator and my cheeks will glow in the central heating. Where will you be? (*Pause.*) You haven't earned the right to laugh at me.

PAUL: Earned the right to feel disappointed. To feel disgusted. Anyway, don't piss all over us with your . . . achievements. Don't piss all over us with what we haven't got.

BENDALL (*furiously, urgently*): You can't keep me here all night you know! The cleaners for a start . . . they'll be here at six. They have their own keys; they'll raise the alarm, scream the fucking house down if they find you here. I'm warning you – the gates will be locked, there'll be no escape!

SAFF: You look a bit tense to me Mr Bendall. A bit anxious, like. I can see your heart bouncing up and down inside your shirt – and you're sweating. Sweat's coming off you like a fucking lawn sprinkler. Roy here was a boxer before law and order got him. You look like you just done three rounds with him.

ROY: He don't look like he's got enough puff to get his dressing-gown off.

SAFF: Trouble with you is pal, you're out of condition. Too many sandwiches sitting on your arse, too many executive lunches – that's your trouble.

ROY: Wish it were mine.

SAFF: You need a bit of a work out. Roy could take you in hand. He's glowing with health, he does press-ups. More stamina than Red Rum. Going places he was – training with the England Squad, semi-finals of the ABAs. He could have been going to Los Angeles in a few years' time – Olympics like.

ROY: But the court said that behaviour like mine couldn't be tolerated in a civilised society. Rid the streets of rampant hooliganism they said. Got a bit angry at a National Front march, see – going through where I lived. Threw a brick at some bloke carrying a Union Jack.

SAFF: In a few years' time in Los Angeles, he could have been following behind someone holding a Union Jack – in his blue blazer and white trousers – marching round the Olympic Stadium. Instead of that he's been shovelling shit in a field and playing ping-pong after supper.

ROY (to PAUL): I used to go every other night. To the club, like. With me Adidas bag. It's the only thing I've ever been any good at. The magistrate reckoned I was a representative of hate and hopelessness. Sounded a bit like him. People like me were sparks in the powderkeg of racial conflict, he reckoned – if it exploded into civil war I'd be responsibile. (To BENDALL:) That ain't fair is it?

BENDALL: Brixton, Bristol, Liverpool – I think your civil war has already started.

PAUL: Spread now though innit. Spread . . . spread here to you!

ROY: I mean though, if a load of guys come down your street shouting 'wogs out' and you happened to be one – a wog like, you'd get a bit fucking angry, right. When hundred skinheads walk down the road with a flag it's a political march innit? When four of us walk down the road, it's stop and search time, y'know.

SAFF (to BENDALL): He could have been representing us – fighting for Great Britain.

ROY: Waving to the crowd.

SAFF: Flashed by satellite back to Stoke Newington. (Using the waste bin as a podium.)

ROY: Fight me heart out. (Standing on the bin.)

SAFF: Beat the Russians and the Americans.

ROY: And the Cubans. Presentation – me on the rostrum. On the top, where it says number one. Hands behind me back, bending down as they put the medal round me neck.

SAFF: The whole country watching – all feeling so patriotic – him being British and everything. Interview with Harry Carpenter afterwards.

ROY: I'd be standing up straight for the National Anthem. Hand on me heart, big grin on me face. Great big grin.

SAFF: That'd be the gumshield still stuck in his mouth.

ROY: God save our gracious queen. Get a tear in me eye, overcome with emotion, like. Recognition after all that sweat, all that dedication.

SAFF: As the Union Jack is raised, so are two fingers.

ROY: An Olympic champion for Britain.

SAFF: When he gets home, the mayor'll wanna congratulate him. Presentation at the Town Hall. He'll get the freedom of Stoke Newington.

ROY: Yeah. Never had it before.

The telephone rings. Pause. They look at each other.

SAFF: Who's this?

BENDALL: Telepathy isn't among my gifts.

ROY: What we going to do – make out we're the Chinese Laundry.

SAFF: You – pick it up! Don't say nothing out of order. Everything's lovely – right! And you're busy, too busy to see anyone. D'you get it? Play the white man or you'll be an hospital case. Go on!

BENDALL (*picking up the receiver*): Hello, John Bendall . . . (*A short pause while he listens.*) No, I'm afraid not. Four you say? No, I've seen nothing at all – I've been stuck in this office all afternoon. I'm in a meeting you see. (*He laughs.*) Better than hanging around on street corners I suppose. (SAFF *reacts.*) I shall probably be leaving a bit later tonight . . . still a few things to go over. Yes, yes – I certainly will. OK, Joe. Cheers. (*Puts it down.*).

SAFF: What was all that about?

BENDALL: That was proof and confirmation that it's unwise for you to be here any longer.

SAFF: Trying to scare us?

ROY: Bluff us.

BENDALL: I am trying to tell you that now would be a good time to bring this shabby little episode to a close.

SAFF: Who was it?

BENDALL: The security guard.

PAUL: Saff . . .

SAFF (*to* PAUL): Wait a minute. (*To* BENDALL:) What's he ringing you up for – wish you happy birthday?

BENDALL: He said that someone had reported four suspicious looking characters hanging around the factory yard. He asked if I'd seen anything.

SAFF: And you said . . .

BENDALL: That I'd keep an eye out.

SAFF: He's got efficient all of a sudden ain't he. We see him fucking off to the betting shop before. What he's after – promotion?

BENDALL: Perhaps he felt guilty and was trying to make amends – not doing his job properly and all that. Like I'm not doing mine at the moment.

SAFF: That security geezer . . . weren't thinking of coming over or nothing?

BENDALL: I couldn't tell you.

SAFF: You better.

BENDALL: He was checking, verifying. But if he's feeling especially conscientious then he may come over to investigate.

PAUL: Investigate what? You told him you was in a meeting. That's what it says on the door. So he ain't got nothing to investigate has he?

ROY: You said something else . . . about staying late.

BENDALL: Well, that depends on you three, doesn't it?

ROY: Your wife might start wondering where you are, your tea'll be getting burned. Here, maybe I could go round and eat it for you. What you got tonight? Boiled fish, chicken kiev, beef bourgignon or steak diane?

SAFF: Steak what?

ROY: Steak diane? That's steak marinated in wine, garlic and mushrooms. (*To* BENDALL:) What d'you think you'll be having for afters. A bit of cheesecake or black forest gateau?

SAFF: Roy, go and get Pimple. Tell him to come in here. You keep look-out.

ROY: Right.

SAFF (*to* BENDALL): What time do the people from the factory outside start going home Mr Bendall?

BENDALL: Five-thirty.

ROY (*going out*): Here – you ever tried duck in orange sauce washed down by a nice fruity beaujolais? (BENDALL *doesn't respond.*) Speak up.

BENDALL: Yes I have. Several times.

ROY (*going out*): What's it like?

PAUL: Yeah, what's it like? What's it like sitting there all day feeling important? (*Pause. To* SAFF.) Why'd you send Roy out there?

SAFF: Pimple might wet himself and run if anyone comes along. Roy won't.

PAUL: You asked him about the people in the factory – what time they went home.

SAFF: I'll tell you why later.

PIMPLE *enters – he is wearing a football scarf over his head, over his face – slits for eyes and mouth.*

PIMPLE: What's been happening?

SAFF: Oh look at him! What d'you think you're doing?

PIMPLE: I've disguised meself.

SAFF: As what?

PIMPLE: I'm anonymous.

SAFF: Fucking hell!

PIMPLE: So that no one can tell who I am.

SAFF (*to* BENDALL): You better watch him. You can tell he's done this sort of thing before can't you. You can tell he's a professional like. I thought it was the fucking elephant man for a minute.

PIMPLE: Well, I thought – I ain't having a photofit picture of me flashed on Police 5. No one can describe me with this over me face.

PAUL: Five foot four and harmless, Pimple.

PIMPLE: Oh fuck!

SAFF: What now?

PIMPLE: He's just mentioned my name. That's a bleeding giveaway that is.

SAFF (*pulling the scarf off*): He's blown your cover! You might as well put your hands up, wave the white flag.

PAUL: That's what he wants me to do – wave a white flag. Give up, go home – try again somewhere else. No more . . . not any more . . .

BENDALL: If you think you're making some kind of stand against me, then your feelings of heroism are sadly misplaced.

PAUL: Don't want to be an hero – just don't want to keep accepting . . . what I'm told. Words like unfortunately and there is no possibility. All means the same though – words like that from people like you. I'm not just a name on a bit of paper that you can put a line through with your pen. Just get me out the way – put me in a file somewhere, in a drawer – keep your distance. (*Pause. To* BENDALL:) The bloke who got the job – you got his application form? All the details on a bit of paper . . . one that didn't have failure written all over it – like mine did.

BENDALL: Your bitterness is beyond me . . . completely. You came for an

interview, you weren't chosen – there's been no travesty of justice, no denial of your human rights. Bad news is all. A setback and nothing more. (*Loudly.*) Surely!

PAUL: Can you get it for me please? His application.

BENDALL: See how it's done eh?

SAFF (*bottle*): Just do it.

BENDALL *goes to the filing cabinet.*

PIMPLE: Here Saff, what did that Roy get put away for?

SAFF: Well, there was this bloke from the National Front. On a march. Roy hurt him with a brick.

PIMPLE: Oh.

SAFF: Should have seen the blood. Supposed to have left him with a face like an half-eaten trifle.

PIMPLE: Bloke from the British Movement eh?

SAFF: Went berserk apparently – Roy did. Hates all them – British Movement, National Front. Gets really violent.

PIMPLE: What d'you tell him about me?

SAFF: What d'you mean?

PIMPLE: You didn't tell him I was in it did you?

SAFF: I might have done. I can't remember.

PIMPLE: Cos I ain't no more. I've left. I have honest. Make sure you tell him. I seen the error of me ways didn't I? I like blacks now – I like 'em a lot. Here, you don't think he'll leave me with a face like a half-eaten trifle do you?

PAUL (*looking at the form of the person taken on*): Wouldn't have taken me too long to learn . . . the basic way . . . pick it up gradual. Get the hang of it. It's only tins of paint innit? I would have applied myself . . . worked me balls off. Make . . . make an effort . . . make a start. (*Talking to* BENDALL, *tearing up the form:*) See . . . forget about him. He ain't on your file no more. He's vanishing . . . thrown him away . . . lost. My turn now, me next – now he's gone. Me next in the queue, my go now please. I'm ready to start . . . soon as you like. No notice to give anyone. Not me.

BENDALL: This is absurd. Ridiculous.

PAUL: I'll show you how absurd it is. (*He takes the bottle from* SAFF.) Take your jacket off.

BENDALL: Deeper and deeper in the shit, my lad.

PAUL: And your tie please.

BENDALL *does both.*

PIMPLE (*giggling*): Right down to his pants.

SAFF *shuts him up.*

PAUL: Put these on Pimple.

PIMPLE: What for?

PAUL: Fancy dress.

PIMPLE: But I ain't going nowhere.

SAFF: Do as you're told.

PIMPLE *puts on the jacket and tie. The jacket is too large, the arms too long. The tie is worn over* PIMPLE'*s T-shirt (V-neck). It is a wide, middle-management tie.*

PAUL: You really look the part.

PIMPLE: What fucking part?

SAFF: You look the business.

PAUL: Businessman.

PIMPLE: What am I supposed to be?

PAUL: You? You're him.

PIMPLE: Him?

PAUL: We'll have a laugh.

SAFF: D'you want him behind the desk?

PAUL (*holds an ashtray over* BENDALL'*s head*): You've come to see Pimple here – about a job you've seen advertised. It's a party game. Right!

PIMPLE: What am I supposed to do then – stand here like this?

PAUL: I told you – you're an high-powered executive. You're him. (*Pause.*) I've come about the job advertised in the local paper.

BENDALL: What?

PAUL: Say it.

BENDALL: I don't believe this is happening!

PAUL: Say it!

BENDALL: I've come . . . I've come about . . . the job advertised in the local paper.

PAUL (*to* PIMPLE): Ask him about his experience.

PIMPLE: What sort of experience?

PAUL: Just ask him.

PIMPLE: You . . . er . . . you got any experience?

PAUL: What about his education?

PIMPLE: Oh yeah – how many 'O' levels you got?

PAUL: Your turn! (*Raising the ashtray again over* BENDALL'*s head.*)

BENDALL: What am I supposed to say!

PAUL: Answer him – you're supposed to be the fucking expert. Go on!

BENDALL: I've got eight 'O' levels . . . similar work . . . I've done similar work.

PIMPLE: Where have you? How long?

PAUL: Speak up!

BENDALL: A paint firm . . . fourteen years.

PAUL: Why's he want the job.

PIMPLE: Yeah?

PAUL: You're desperate ain't you? Ain't you!

BENDALL: I'm desperate.

PAUL: Cos you got made redundant.

BENDALL: Redundant . . . yes.

PAUL: Out of work for eighteen months.

BENDALL: Out of work . . . for eighteen months.

PAUL: Just like me. You're at the end of your tether.

BENDALL: I'm at . . . I'm at the end . . . the end of my tether. (*Pointedly.*)

PAUL: You've looked everywhere for work – can't face another day like this. Your whole life is becoming a waste. A waste!

BENDALL: A waste. (*With sarcasm.*)

PAUL: A wasted life!

BENDALL: A wasted life. (*Ironic.*)

PAUL: Guess who you're playing!

BENDALL: My God this is out of control! My God it is!

PAUL *breaks off.* BENDALL *is almost breathless.*

PAUL: Ask him why he's dressed like that. Supposed to look smart when you go for interviews.

PIMPLE (*becoming a bit anxious*): Might as well stop this now eh Paul – take this jacket off. Don't fit anyway. I'm supposed to be the look-out anyway. that's why I come. Just be the look-out, weren't it?

PAUL: Ask him like I said.

Pause. PIMPLE *is uncomfortable.*

PIMPLE: Er . . . bit scruffy ain't you?

PAUL: Explain yourself.

BENDALL (*emotionally*): Haven't you had enough?

PAUL: Explain yourself.

BENDALL: Stolen . . . my jacket was stolen.

SAFF: What d'you think . . . you going to take him on?

PIMPLE: Nah – he's got shifty eyes. Looks like he'd have his hand in the till.

PAUL: You've failed I'm afraid. You've been unsuccessful. You ain't up to standard.

BENDALL *spits in* PAUL's *face.* SAFF *is waiting for* PAUL's *reaction. Pause.* PAUL *wipes his face, looks at* BENDALL.

That was a laugh, weren't it.

PIMPLE: Shall I give him his jacket and tie back?

PAUL: Might as well. (*A bit subdued.*)

BENDALL *is putting on his tie.*

PIMPLE: We leaving in a minute then?

SAFF: Not long.

PIMPLE: What was it like, Saff – being put away?

SAFF: Weren't Pontins.

PIMPLE: Did you get homesick?

SAFF: No – I got borstal sick. Sick of borstal. Their idea of reforming you was to get you pulling potatoes out the mud or making you run through it in your shorts when it was freezing cold. Yeah, get the snot running down our chins and our balls turnings to brass, they thought we'd all leave there wanting to be Lord Mayors.

PIMPLE: Were the geezers hard in there?

SAFF: Even the fucking cook was hard, Pimple. Clamping down on you little bastards now, one of the screws inside reckoned. Cos of what happened in the summer – all that aggravation. Drop a pint of milk now and you'll get a plastic bullet up your arse.

During this conversation, BENDALL *has picked up his jacket, is brushing it down.*

In Slough, best thing was to have a job in the laundry. Clean and warm in there.

BENDALL *suddenly flings his jacket at the boys. Goes for the fire alarm.*

BENDALL: Right – time's up! Don't move, don't even fart or I'll smash this. OK!

PIMPLE: It's the fire alarm. He's going to set it off!

SAFF (*to* PIMPLE): Stay where you are!

BENDALL: That's it sonny! Stay where you are! If the glass goes on this it'll sound like the four minute warning! Place'll erupt like fucking Wembley Stadium! Fancy that do we?

SAFF: Lot of people running about?

BENDAL: Bloody right!

PIMPLE: Don't do it mister – they'll put me away, they'll clamp down on me! I'll get homesick, I'll get beat up! Even the cook's hard, mister. Let us go will ya!

SAFF: Stop panicking, you.

PAUL: I'm sorry Saff. Should never have . . .

BENDALL: My turn to do the talking, your turn to squirm, Mr Unemployed 1981. I've stuck your utterances for long enough . . . you and your band of merry men . . . society's lepers and losers. Victims of the age my arse. Asking me to change my mind . . . in favour of you! You couldn't even wipe your nose without instructions – the fine young men whose only argument is a broken bottle, who air their grievances by kicking heads in! And you turn up here with a mouthful of animosity, you scum . . .

SAFF: We'll just be leaving then.

PIMPLE: I ain't even supposed to be here mister, I'm supposed to be learning how to paint walls. Don't do nothing eh mister? They'll send me to Slough, I won't even get a job in the laundry.

BENDALL: Shut up you little tike, shut up!

SAFF: He don't want to end up on the scrap-heap.

BENDALL: You'll go when I say now – otherwise I set this fucking thing off! What the hell gives you the right to come here demanding my attention, expecting my help? But then your generation is very good at demanding this and expecting that. Like newly hatched birds with their mouths wide open waiting for their mothers to feed them worms. I want, I need, I expect! And if you can't get it – complain and whine. The basic psychology of all your lot. Complain about your comprehensive education, whine about your council estate existences. Any excuse to explain your thuggery.

PAUL: Waste of time complaining . . . nothing changes.

BENDALL: Oh yes, we have a new development now don't we? Screw initiative, screw responsibility. You're part of the crew that burns down shops and turns over cars when it gets fed up complaining.

PAUL: How do you know what I am? What I'm part of?

BENDALL: This afternoon's display . . . that's how I know. You've brought that stinking behaviour here. This has been nothing less than a fucking trial! The civil war had spread, you were gloating, that came from your own lips, chummy!

PAUL: People took notice . . . when the kids was on the streets . . . your lot . . . for a little while. Then they forgot . . . something different on the front page . . . Royal Wedding.

BENDALL: Leave. Now. Piss off. Vanish. You smell and your lives smell. Make it fast or I'll break the glass, the alarm will scream and they'll all come running! Hand over the money and the cards before you leave too. Put them down there.

SAFF (doing so): D'you want your luncheon vouchers as well?

BENDALL: I don't have to listen to your jokes now you bastard.

SAFF (bending down to put them on the floor): You've made a bit of a mistake here. I'm surprised you ain't spotted it. See, if you do set off the alarm, there might be a lot of puffing and panting down the fire escape, a lot of commotion and the security guard will probably be round but we'll get lost in the rush. Anonymous, like. You won't be rushing nowhere. I've still got this see. (He produces the bottle.) And to be honest, it don't matter a fuck to me if the bells start ringing – I'll leave you looking like a side of beef before I go. If you believe me, you better come away from there.

BENDALL: You'd attack me gratuitously, is that what you're saying?

SAFF: I think so. Yeah, what I'm saying is – if you do get the fire brigade charging round here, the only job they'll have will be mopping up your blood.

BENDALL: I really think you mean it!

SAFF (loudly): Course I fucking mean it! (Holding the knife against BENDALL's throat.)

PAUL: Leave your face looking like one of them Picasso paintings.

SAFF: If you come away from there, if you behave yourself – there won't be any bother.

BENDALL: No retaliation?

SAFF: Best mates.

BENDALL (moving away slowly): What kind of people are you? How did you evolve into what you are?

SAFF: We're good to our mothers.

BENDALL: This hatred, this abuse – is . . . unnatural . . . illogical . . . vicious.

PAUL: You could have given me a bit of hope, shown me . . . belief. You could have made a big difference to my life – you was just going through the motions though. Read this, sign that. Ask a few questions. Not good enough – next please. All in a day's work, right?

PIMPLE: Can I go outside and be look-out again, Saff? I'm better at that. I'm good at being look-out. Sharp eyes, know what I mean?

SAFF: Yeah all right – don't try and leg it through the gates though will ya? The geezer in the uniform'll be on to us then. And I'll give 'em your name and address if we get caught.

PIMPLE: No, I won't go nowhere. Honest. I weren't really scared then. I weren't.

SAFF: You was just making out weren't you?

PIMPLE: Yeah.

SAFF: Get Roy in here.

PIMPLE: Yeah right. See you later then. See you Paul. (*To* BENDALL.) Ta-ta then.

Pause.

BENDALL: What now? For Christ's sake what now!

ROY *enters.*

ROY: Been having trouble?

SAFF: He thought there was going to be a fire, but then he changed his mind.

ROY: Yeah, I know, your little mate Pimple told me. He seemed a bit nervous, he kept twitching. He kept saying something about a face like a half-eaten trifle.

SAFF: Don't worry about him, he's just highly strung.

ROY: Anyone worked out how we're going to get out of here with no hassle?

SAFF: I have. (*Pause.*) Mr Bendall has just been telling us what he thinks of us. Scum and lepers and losers, he reckons.

PAUL: Never said all that this morning. Not out loud anyway. Different this morning though. Handshakes and diplomacy. Seen his disgust now.

BENDALL: Whatever I've got I'll never have your propensity to enjoy hurting people.

SAFF: I bet the only thing he's ever hit is a golf ball. You ever played golf Roy?

ROY: Not many golf courses in Stoke Newington.

SAFF: Not much of fuck all in Stoke Newington, I always thought.

ROY: Don't get a lot of tourists there if that's what you mean.

SAFF: I heard that Brixton is getting a lot of tourists now and they're all fucking MPs.

ROY: All come to wag their fingers.

SAFF: What – when Christmas come early?

ROY: You get fed up with window shopping all the time.

PAUL: Different in July though.

ROY: Only place that didn't get touched was the Jobcentre, that's cos everyone knew it had fuck all to offer.

PAUL: Yeah – but I thought it might be better news today. I'm going outside a minute, Saff.

SAFF: What for?

PAUL: I won't be long. Just be outside by the corridor with Pimple.

SAFF: Tell Pimple there's a closed circuit telly hid behind the plants and they've got ten minutes of him on film. He'll be shitting Mars Bars.

PAUL *goes out.*

Cosy innit?

ROY: How much longer d'you reckon we'll have to stay?

SAFF: The people in the factory finish at half past. We'll leave when they do – walk through the gates in the crowd right? And it's dark outside – no one is going to notice us.

ROY: What if he rings up the security man soon as we leave?

SAFF: Depends how we leave him.

BENDALL: What do you mean? What do you mean by that?

SAFF *ignores him.*

ROY: They're going to do Paul anyway – trespass and threatening behaviour. He's going to end up in the same place we just run away from.

SAFF: He ain't thinking about that is he? All up here with him. But he can be wicked as well. We had a fight once. I wound up with eight stitches in me head. (*Pause.*) Anyway, he's done us a good favour, bringing us here.

ROY: Shall we try and get down to the coast?

SAFF: I ain't fussy. World's our oyster innit?

ROY: Yeah, all slimy and sickly.

SAFF: We'll go down to the seaside then. Stay in one of them guest houses.

ROY: Mr and Mrs Smith.

SAFF: Paul was always going on about the seaside. Getting away to Folkestone.

ROY: We might take him with us, yeah.

SAFF: Tell you what – why don't we hire a coach and have a fucking beano.

ROY: They're going to catch us ain't they – in the end. Send us back. Be worse then I reckon.

SAFF: Don't talk like that! You wanted to get away as bad as me. Cut your hair, take your clothes away and inspect your arsehole – and that's just the first hour. They read me mum's letters, blew whistles at me all day and kicked me and called me a cunt 'cos me laces come undone. Fuck their hospitality.

ROY: That's how they teach you respect for law and order. Set an example like.

BENDALL: Listen . . . I've a meeting to go to. It's absolutely essential that . . . that I attend.

SAFF: You don't give up do you? Anyway, what's wrong with this meeting.

BENDALL: You don't understand . . . they'll be expecting me – I've got a paper to present to them. They'll be phoning to see where I've got to.

SAFF: I ain't swallowing that one, Bendall.

ROY: Yeah, we weren't born yesterday. (*Dryly.*) Didn't come over on the banana boat you know.

SAFF: Bit late to go to a meeting.

BENDALL: From time to time . . . in my job . . . I am required to work into the evening. They'll be waiting for me I tell you.

SAFF: My dad always said you office bastards never do any overtime. You don't need to.

BENDALL: I'll be receiving a phone call shortly . . . you can be assured of that. What am I going to say?

SAFF: Sit still Bendall. Or I'll get Roy to use your nose as his speedball. Be a bit of training for him.

ROY: Missed out on all that these past months. Lose a lot of your timing and forget your moves and your shots. When I think about all the sparring I ain't had and the bouts I might have fought – seems like a right waste. (*Pause.*) Gotta make a go of it one day, 'cos otherwise there's nothing. (*Pause.*) London team went to Florence in August to box. I should have been going. All expenses paid an all.

SAFF: Shouldn't throw bricks at the National Front should ya?

ROY: Nah – I suppose I should have invited 'em in for a cup of tea, yeah. Been polite. (*Pause.*) At the club right, it didn't matter what colour you was. I really used to like going there – it was like a big family sort of – timing each other on the circuits, going running together and trying out moves in the ring. All mates then y'know – like going to places together on the coach and cheering each other on when we're fighting. Right close – weren't no differences between black guys and white – you all shared the same club colours, shared the same showers. All boxers right – all learning and sweating and moaning about how hard George used to make us train. Great atmosphere on busy nights – really friendly. But when you go outside in the street, people call you spade and there's slogans up on the walls. If everywhere was like the club, be all right.

SAFF: Me and you got friendly in Slough though. I mean, everyone thinks we've done a bunk but really we've fucking eloped ain't we. Hand in hand.

ROY: That why you wanna get me in one of them guest houses by the seaside.

SAFF: Course. But what I was saying . . . about Slough – it's right though innit? Cos it was rough down there and we was all in bother . . . well, you team up together. Black and white – it don't make no odds. Cos you all know that it's the screws who's the enemy. Like on the outside as well, kids tearing out each other's throats – that's cos they don't know who their real enemies are.

PAUL *has come in near the beginning of* SAFF*'s speech.* SAFF *sees him, carries on talking.* PAUL *is in overalls or preferably a brown factory-type coat.*

PAUL: He's not my enemy. Not him. I'm counting on him.

SAFF: Where d'you get that?

PAUL: He can tell you.

BENDALL: The small stockroom down the corridor. He must have broken in.

PAUL: Didn't need to. Key was in the lock. Suits me don't it.

BENDALL: Is this another game.

PAUL: Is this what I'd be wearing – in the stockroom, like? Is this standard gear – for being a stockroom assistant. Factory regulations is it? (*Pause.*) Talk to me then.

BENDALL (*warily*): Health and safety legislation, yes.

PAUL: I think it's very becoming meself.

SAFF (*unsure himself but playing along*): Makes you look all efficient.

PAUL: Pockets as well. Would I have a locker to hang it up in? I suppose it'd get dirty – what with all the dust and oil and paint. But that's what it's for innit – to get dirty. Fits me though. Perfect. Anyone'd think it had been especially made for me. All I need now is a clipboard and I'd be all set to go.

BENDALL (*to the other two*): Look, what's his game, what's he on about? Do either of you two know what he's doing?

PAUL: I see the boys coming home from Barclays Bank sometimes. They have squash rackets in their bags. Play during lunchtimes, like. Nice.

BENDALL: In an ideal world I wouldn't have to say no to anyone but it's not and I do.

PAUL: All them MPs cheering and booing in the House of Commons – tell 'em to set up another committee, another inquiry. And you here couldn't even be bothered to read my references.

BENDALL: Look, there are no magic solutions and I'm only the lousy personnel manager for Christ's sake!

PAUL (*pulling out rope; quiet, strange sort of calmness*): Found this in there. Nylon it is. That's what they use now. Funny how you don't see the old sort, anymore. The sort they used to have on the docks. The blokes from the ships used to throw them out to be tied round the capstans. Rougher than nylon. Nice smell they had though – smelled old – the sea and sweaty hands and horses and faraway places. When I used to hear the hooters in the middle of the night, I used to wish I could be on one of those ships going across to the other side of the world. No more hooters, no more old rope.

SAFF (*incredulous*): Paul – what's going on? What's that for?

PAUL: He was saying about a trial before weren't he? This is nothing less than a fucking trial he said. Well, d'you think he's guilty?

ROY: Heavy!

SAFF: What you saying Paul – don't talk silly . . .

BENDALL: He's . . . he's not intending . . . I hope this isn't . . . this isn't some sick plan to scare me. Have you planned this?

PAUL: Guilty.

BENDALL: My God he's crazy! He's a bloody raving lunatic! Stop him, get that rope away from him! Look, I'll speak up for you two, I'll say you were forced into coming here – against your will. He'll make things worse for both of you. You can't let him get away with this.

PAUL: The sentence of this court . . .

SAFF: Paul, you winding us up? Something you thought up outside? It's worked anyway. He's cracking up.

PAUL: Passing sentence. He judged me . . . a failure. Now I judge him. I mean it.

SAFF: We've rolled the fucker, don't want to bury him. You are joking.

PAUL: I'll manage on me own.

BENDALL: Look, you can have this (*His watch.*) quartz timing, gold strap. You'll have no trouble getting rid of it. And these too – gold cufflinks . . . wedding present . . . engraved. Worth about £200. Get that bloody rope away from him.

PAUL: By his neck.

ROY: He'd do it, he'd fucking do it Saff!

SAFF: Stop talking like that will you. We'll be away in a minute when they come out the factory. Give us that, yeah.

ROY: Have to fight him for it.

PIMPLE (*putting his head round the door*): Everyone's going home! Bloke in the uniform is fucking coming across the yard!

ROY: We'd better go down the corridor and out through the main yard. Like now Saff!

SAFF: Gotta forget it now Paul. (*He takes PAUL by the arm.*)

PAUL: Can't forget.

ROY: Sorry Paul – we gotta leave. Split.

SAFF (*to ROY*): Take Pimple with you – be there in a minute. Mind yourself right!

ROY *and* PIMPLE *go.*

You wanna end up like me Paul, you wanna fuck your life up?

PAUL: It's already fucked up.

SAFF: You got to get out of here! So what if he don't understand, if he thinks we're dirt. Him and his kind are good at calling us names, good at dealing with us, like they dealt with me and Roy. But you're different to the rest of us, Paul, you don't deserve the names they're going to call you and the borstal they're going to give you. He ain't worth it.

PAUL: See you later.

SAFF: I got to catch the others up. Still on the fucking run ain't I? Last time Paul, for fuck's sake.

PAUL: Leave us now Saff.

SAFF: Thick as thieves, right?

PAUL: Yeah.

SAFF *goes.*

BENDALL: Look, I think I can help you. I'll write you a letter of recommendation, that's what I'll do – for other employers in the area. A letter of recommendation signed by me . . . to present at interviews.

During the following, PAUL gets a chair, attaches the rope to a beam, tying a crude noose, and gets down.

PAUL: No problem now, I won't be a problem. Be out of everybody's way. I won't need help no more – no one has to worry about me . . . nor will I. I don't have to get disgusted no more. All over now, all over.

Lights dim. Black.

Music, very loud: 'Enjoy Yourself by The Specials.

Royal Court Writers Series.

THE SEAGULL
by Anton Chekhov (in a new version by Thomas Kilroy)
NOT QUITE JERUSALEM
by Paul Kember
BORDERLINE
by Hanif Kureishi
TOUCHED
TIBETAN INROADS
by Stephen Lowe
OPERATION BAD APPLE
by G. F. Newman

RSC Pit Playtexts

MONEY
by Edward Bulwer-Lytton
OUR FRIENDS IN THE NORTH
by Peter Flannery
A DOLL'S HOUSE
by Henrik Ibsen (translated by Michael Meyer)

The Master Playwrights

Collections of plays by the best-known modern playwrights in value-for-money paperbacks.

John Arden	PLAYS: ONE
	Serjeant Musgrave's Dance, The Workhouse Donkey, Armstrong's Last Goodnight
Brendan Behan	THE COMPLETE PLAYS
	The Hostage, The Quare Fellow, Richard's Cork Leg, Moving Out, A Garden Party, The Big House
Edward Bond	PLAYS: ONE
	Saved, Early Morning, The Pope's Wedding
	PLAYS: TWO
	Lear, The Sea, Narrow Road to the Deep North, Black Mass, Passion
Noël Coward	PLAYS: ONE
	Hay Fever, The Vortex, Fallen Angels, Easy Virtue
	PLAYS: TWO
	Private Lives, Bitter Sweet, The Marquise, Post-Mortem
	PLAYS: THREE
	Design for Living, Cavalcade, Conversation Piece and *Hands Across the Sea, Still Life* and *Fumed Oak from Tonight at 8.30*
	PLAYS: FOUR
	Blithe Spirit, This Happy Breed, Present Laughter, and *Ways and Means, The Astonished Heart* and *Red Peppers from Tonight at 8.30*
Henrik Ibsen	*Translated and introduced by Michael Meyer*
	PLAYS: ONE
	Ghosts, The Wild Duck, The Master Builder
	PLAYS: TWO
	A Doll's House, An Enemy of the People, Hedda Gabler
	PLAYS: THREE
	Rosmersholm, Little Eyolf, The Lady from the Sea
	PLAYS: FOUR
	John Gabriel Borkman, The Pillars of Society, When We Dead Awaken
Joe Orton	THE COMPLETE PLAYS
	Entertaining Mr Sloane, Loot, What the Butler Saw, The Ruffian on the Stair, The Epringham Camp, Funeral Games, The Good and Faithful Servant
Harold Pinter	PLAYS: ONE
	The Birthday Party, The Room, The Dumb Waiter, A Slight Ache, A Night Out
	PLAYS: TWO
	The Caretaker, Night School, The Dwarfs, The Collection, The Lover, five revue sketches
	PLAYS: THREE
	The Homecoming, Tea Party, The Basement, Landscape, Silence, six revue sketches
	PLAYS: FOUR
	Old Times, No Man's Land, Betrayal, Monologue, Family Voices
Terence Rattigan	PLAYS: ONE
	French Without Tears, The Winslow Boy, The Browning Version, Harlequinade